PSYCHOLOGY, PUNITIVE ACTIVATION AND WELFARE

This book explores welfare politics, unemployment and interventions in relation to the labour market. Using critical fieldwork and theory, the author explores the administration of the unemployed, and the drive to increase labour market participation through strategies of activation.

There is a strong and coherent conceptual framing for this work with critique taking centre stage. This book will introduce readers to new approaches to researching unemployment in the productive spaces between critical fieldwork and critical theory. The innovative 'post-disciplinary' approach is committed to uncovering, understanding and resisting how people's lives are undone and then remade in contemporary welfare regimes.

Psychology, Punitive Activation and Welfare will appeal to students engaging with critical psychology, unemployment or policy, by providing a distinct application of theoretical and methodological tools to think differently about the relationship between labour market non/participation, human misery, psychology, frontline enactment of policy and research.

Rose-Marie Stambe is a Postdoctoral Research Fellow in the School of Social Sciences at the University of Queensland, Australia. Her main research interests are in critical qualitative methodology, the welfare-work nexus, social disadvantage and subjectivity.

Concepts for Critical Psychology: Disciplinary Boundaries Re-thought
Series editor: Ian Parker

Developments inside psychology that question the history of the discipline and the way it functions in society have led many psychologists to look outside the discipline for new ideas. This series draws on cutting-edge critiques from just outside psychology in order to complement and question critical arguments emerging inside. The authors provide new perspectives on subjectivity from disciplinary debates and cultural phenomena adjacent to traditional studies of the individual.

The books in the series are useful for advanced-level undergraduate and postgraduate students, researchers and lecturers in psychology and other related disciplines such as cultural studies, geography, literary theory, philosophy, psychotherapy, social work and sociology.

Most recently published titles:

Internet Addiction
A Critical Psychology of Users
Emaline Friedman

Radio Activism
Breaking the Silence and Empowering Women
Annette Rimmer

The Event of Psychopoetics
Imagination and the Rupture of Psychology
Raúl García

Psychogeography and Psychology
In and beyond the Discipline
Alex J. Bridger

A Critical Reflexive Approach to Sex Research
Interviews with Men Who Pay for Sex
Monique Huysamen

Psychology, Punitive Activation and Welfare
Blaming the Unemployed
Rose-Marie Stambe

PSYCHOLOGY, PUNITIVE ACTIVATION AND WELFARE

Blaming the Unemployed

Rose-Marie Stambe

Routledge
Taylor & Francis Group
LONDON AND NEW YORK

Cover image: © Getty Images

First published 2022
by Routledge
4 Park Square, Milton Park, Abingdon, Oxon OX14 4RN

and by Routledge
605 Third Avenue, New York, NY 10158

Routledge is an imprint of the Taylor & Francis Group, an informa business

British Library Cataloguing-in-Publication Data
A catalogue record for this book is available from the British Library

Library of Congress Cataloguing-in-Publication Data
A catalog record has been requested for this book

ISBN: 978-0-367-63224-3 (hbk)
ISBN: 978-0-367-63222-9 (pbk)
ISBN: 978-1-003-11251-8 (ebk)

DOI: 10.4324/9781003112518

Typeset in Bembo
by MPS Limited, Dehradun

For James and Archie.

CONTENTS

FIGURE

SERIES PREFACE

We all work. The analysis and argument in this pressing pertinent book is for those who think they are secure in employment, for they sense day-by-day the precarity of their position, and for those who are told they are not working because they are not employed. Rose Stambe lays bare the mechanisms by which we are increasingly subject to regimes of work that operate according to what the historian and philosopher Michel Foucault called 'dividing practices'; here forms of separation that divide those who really 'work' – those who labour for a wage, are exploited, those from whom surplus value is extracted – and those who are feckless, unproductive, wasteful.

The key mechanisms call upon psychology and instil psychology; they require the disciplinary apparatus that measures and regulates and separates categories of person, and they function by inciting a 'psychological' sense in each of us, that the conditions we face are, when it comes down to it, our own fault. Psychology is embedded in the interior of each human subject under capitalism through what is artfully described here as 'punitive activation'. The conditions of possibility for this punitive activation are today 'neoliberal'. Neoliberalism is in some ways a return to the earliest most unfeeling days of classical liberal capitalist political economy, but with a difference, the difference that the growth of psychology makes.

First, an often neglected element of neoliberalism is the intensification of the kind of processes of discipline that Foucault registered in his work on prisons and on contemporary society configured as if it were a prison; that intensification is present in the most obvious growth and abuse of state power in neoliberal experiments after military coups or invasion, with Chile in September 1973 one first terrible warning. Neoliberalism requires a strong state and an atmosphere of fear, but that fear works its way down into everyday life, and is present now in the democracies, with Australia in this book being a case in point; regimes of fear to which the 'unemployed' are subject are undergirded by punishment for infraction of welfare rules. A second more obvious element of neoliberalism is the intensification of competitive individualism so that societal and collective support is stripped away and each individual is made to face their conditions of life alone, told to deal with it, told to be 'responsible' for what they have brought upon themselves. This is the world that the discipline of psychology operates in, observing, recording, theorising about the nature of this individual abstracted from social context.

The third element is the focus of this book, but the book makes clear that this third element is only able to operate against the background of the first two. The third element is the crucial difference that psychology makes, enables, activates as never before. Yes, we were always told that it was our fault if bad things happen to us, but psychologisation in the welfare system drums in the moral lesson that you must feel this fault at depth and work on it. You must work, engage in psychological work, know in the core of your self that this desperate state of unemployment is down to you. You might look across the boundary, the other side of the dividing practice that separates you from those precarious souls who are employed, perhaps on short-term 'zero' contracts, and they will be looking across at the unemployed, wondering how long it will be before they are there too. Contemporary neoliberal life, this book shows us, is about forms of work, psychological work among those who are employed and those who are not, neither directly inside nor outside paid work, but 'outwith' it. This book is, among other things, about the reproduction of psychology at times of crisis, providing an analysis that might help us refuse it.

Ian Parker
University of Manchester

ACKNOWLEDGEMENTS

I never would have made it this far without the support and encouragement of many. I'm grateful to each person but I'd like to acknowledge a notable few here. I'd like to thank the employment consultants who participated in my research despite the time pressures of their work. I'd like to thank the unemployed clients who took time to chat even though by talking to me they were unnecessarily extending the time spent in employment services. These conversations didn't directly inform this study but have greatly influenced how I think about, and would like to rethink, unemployment.

I would like to thank my colleagues at the University of Queensland and beyond, including David Fryer, Ravinder Sidhu, Silke Meyer, Greg Marston, Ian Parker and Kerry Chamberlain. Your generous and constructive feedback helped shape the research and this book and will continue to influence my thinking. I'd also like to thank Ian Parker for believing in the manuscript and the reviewers whose insightful suggestions improved this work. Thank you to my peers who provided stimulating conversations that helped my thinking and whose friendship is a welcome relief from the academic/research assemblage, namely: Laura Cox, Amir Salimiha, Agnieszka Sobolewska, Charles Marley, Angelina Tang, Rachael Fox, Madonna Boman, Lisa Pope, Cameron Parsell and Hanne Worsoe. A particular thank you to Agnieszka Sobolewska, Ravinder Sidhu, Hanne Worsoe and Kate Boshier who were patient and generous enough to read and edit earlier versions of this book.

I'd like to thank my family and friends for their love, support and encouragement. And, finally, to James and Archie, I love you to the moon and back. This research was supported by an Australian Government Research Training Program Scholarship.

ABBREVIATIONS

ES	Employment services
ES1	East site 1
GROUP	Group case management
JSA	Job Services Australia
JN	Job Network
LEC	Lead employment consultant
MO	Mutual obligations
NAR	Non-attendance report
NS1	North site 1
NS2	North site 2
PIA	Poststructural interview analysis
SDP	Service delivery plan
SS1	South site 1
WfD	Work for the Dole
WPR	What's the problem (represented to be)?
WS1	West site 1

1

INTRODUCTION

Introduction

At the time of writing this introduction, the novel coronavirus (COVID-19) was still having considerable ramifications for countries around the world. The virus reshaped the political, economic and social landscape of many countries, with public health orders restricting economic activity leading to higher un(der)employment. Measures taken to address the pandemic before vaccines were made disrupted global supply chains, movement of people and local economies. Unemployment and underemployment increased dramatically across the globe (International Labor Organisation [ILO], 2020). In Australia, where I live, social distancing measures initiated in March 2020 stopped nearly 1 million Australians from working (Hayne, 2020). By the end of April 2020, 587,686 applications had been processed for the unemployment payment (Job Seeker payment, formerly Newstart), which is more than what is processed in one year (Office of the Prime Minister [OPM], 2020).

In July 2020, the Australian unemployment rate was 7.4%, and underemployment was at 11.7%. These figures do not incorporate the 'discouraged' who have dropped out of the labour market because they have stopped actively looking for a job, meaning that the number of people who consider themselves to be unemployed was much higher (Coates et al., 2020). These unemployment figures are dwarfed by numbers in different parts of the world, for example, the unemployment rate in South Africa was 30.1% in the first quarter of 2020 (Statistics South Africa, 2020). There are many important arguments to make in relation to how unemployment figures are counted, the social, economic and political context where numbers are counted, and how the unemployment figure functions. This includes political and economic constructions of unemployment and how it relates to 'calculating' and 'managing' inflation and the implications of

DOI: 10.4324/9781003112518-1

having a certain 'active' group of unemployed 'count' (Baxandall, 2002; Stambe & Fryer, 2015). I will not revisit these concerns in this book. Instead, I want to unsettle any easy readings of what 'unemployment' is, why it is a problem, and reconsider the role of psychology and research regardless of the official unemployment figure.

Welfare regimes, COVID and the psy-complex

The welfare policies of OECD-member countries have been characterised by increasing conditionality, underpinned by the notion of 'activation' that became dominant from the 1990s (Moreira & Lødemel, 2014). The administration of the unemployed has been placed at the centre of employment policies, shifting concerns from labour demand to labour supply. The governmental focus shifted to 'activating' individuals to maintain job search and improve their employability despite labour market conditions. Governments intervene on the market aiming for an 'active society' where individuals are responsibilised to ensure their own wellbeing. In the context of Employment Services (ES), the organisations that in various policy contexts are supposed to activate the unemployed, that wellbeing is operationalised as getting a job. As succinctly explained by a former Australian Prime Minister, the "best form of welfare is a job" (Abbott, 2015). The behaviour and emotional lives of the unemployed are now the targets of policy. Activation strategies involve a combination of carrots and sticks, such as job search clubs, vocational skills training and sanctions to ensure job seekers are attached to the labour market, supposedly providing a surplus of motivated and job-ready labour.

In an Australian context, ES is a conglomerate of for-profit and not-for-profit organisations, or 'Providers', that are contracted by the Australian Government to 'activate' the unemployed. The current model is called *jobactive* and involves activation strategies that are designed to 'encourage' job seekers to persist with job search despite labour market conditions. The increasingly punitive nature of activation and the refusal to adequately raise social security payments reflects a general policy shift away from the original welfare policy objectives to alleviate poverty towards a more neoliberalised focus on labour market participation. Similar trajectories that prioritise coercive behaviouralism are occurring in other countries such as the USA, the United Kingdom and Aotearoa/New Zealand (Abramovitz, 2006; Wright et al., 2020, Ware et al., 2017). In some OECD contexts (see Friedli & Stern, 2015; Yang, 2015; Pultz, 2018), psychologised discourses provide the expertise and common sense to justify and authorise many of these practices that, as I argue in this book, function to blame the unemployed for their unemployment.

This book was built around research that I did in 2015 and 2016 in South East Queensland. It was a quasi-ethnographic study that brought together a critical reading of policy, interviews with employment consultants and observations of the service delivery model of one ES provider that I've named 'Active Job'. The research aim was to highlight how the unemployed are produced as such through the practices used to govern them. Namely, I studied how unemployment was produced as a problem of the unemployed who required reformation into an affective subject ready to withstand the ebbs and flows of the market. This research also extended methodological debates in governmentality studies by attuning the research focus onto how methods, especially the interview, are implicated in the power-knowledge nexus. I wanted to develop a 'post-disciplinary' approach to research unemployment; to rethink the study of unemployment/unemployed as an 'object' and take a more critical attitude to the question, *how* should we study unemployment?

Then the pandemic happened. In Australia, as in many other OECD countries, the Government response to suppress the COVID-19 reshaped the policy, legal, political and economic landscape. Like other states, the Australian Government did something that seemed extraordinary. The neoliberal-influenced policies that I briefly described above, which have endured over decades and resisted any meaningful revision (Watts, 2016), were dramatically altered almost overnight. The federal government introduced a quasi-wage subsidy program to keep people employed, added a COVID-19 supplement to increase Job Seeker payments, which doubled the payment despite having refused to raise the rate in real terms for more than 20 years (Australian Counsil of Social Services [ACOSS], 2020), and suspended welfare conditions (known as mutual obligations, MO). Nevertheless, the Australian Government was determined to return to business as usual and these initiatives have been phased out.

Simultaneously, the uniqueness of this 'quarantine unemployment' changed some of the public discourse about worklessness. Unemployment was catapulted into the headlines and it appeared as though the public conversation about unemployment had shifted. Previous to the pandemic, media representations of unemployment were generally limited to depictions of the lazy undeserving poor (Gibson, 2009; Nolan, 2003). These stories of the 'welfare bludger' have long histories in a Global North welfare context, particularly in Australia (Klein, 2020), the United Kingdom (Walters, 2000) and the United States (Fraser & Gordon, 1994). The pandemic changed the tone to empathy, repeating known 'truths' about the negative impact of unemployment on the individual. For example, when the United Statesian Alex Reiff confessed on his LinkedIn account that he has lost his job, identity and sense of worth, the Australian media ran a story about the 'viral' post alongside the advice from a psychologist who posited the 'truth' that being unemployed is a financial and psychological blow, "when you lose a job, you're obviously losing an income, but you're also losing a way of [navigating] the world" (Kesley-Sugg & Tickle, 2020). These narratives that explore the angst of the unemployed mirror a 'truth' in advanced liberalism – that unemployment *causes* ill-being.

Here the psy-complex finds a renewed sense of authority in relation to unemployment. The 'psy-complex' is a network of relations, about psychological knowledges which are made into 'common sense' in the public domain (Parker, 1997) and become ingrained as regular ways of talking about oneself and others

(Rose, 1996). It becomes the foundational source for understanding how unemployment 'feels', and how best to manage and cope in order to 'bounce back'. I find the individualising and pathologising impact of psychological theory, research and practices inadequate to explain and 'intervene' in this area of 'unemployment'. How can we reduce such a complex social phenomenon that serves multiple purposes to be an issue of cognitions, mindsets, coping strategies or personality traits? Moreover, how do these knowledges function in contemporary welfare regimes that are increasingly punitive? How can we research unemployment without reproducing such individualised notions of unemployment? In this book, I present an argument that the unemployed are blamed for their misery, which is constituted through the network of political, economic, social, psychological and research practices. Rather than resort to psychologised notions of self and wellbeing, we need to reimagine how we think about and research unemployment.

A 'post-disciplinary' approach to unemployment

A critical psychological approach to researching unemployment is a small area with few researchers explicitly taking such a perspective (see Blustein et al., 2012; Fryer & Stambe, 2014a; 2014b; for a community critical perspective see Fryer, 2012). This body of work mostly covers theoretical components using Foucault, to describe psychological notions of unemployment within neoliberalism. Others have engaged in Foucauldian-inspired research, usually applying governmentality to critique psychological knowledges in ES (Cromby & Willis, 2014; Drewery, 1998; Friedli & Stern, 2015; Pultz, 2018). This book extends on this literature by incorporating the trend in governmentality studies to use social science fieldwork practices to attend to the messiness of policy enactment in situ, including how neoliberal discourses sit alongside, clash and contradict with other discourses and problematisations (Walkerdine & Bansel, 2010). Attending to the implications of governing practices also requires examining the productivity of research practices. Research should seriously examine what types of problems are assumed and produced through the research process, and which concepts are left self-evident and unproblematised.

For this book, I utilised a Foucauldian-inspired bricolage as one way of researching unemployment in an Australian context. I reconsider how research can reconnect the economic, political, institutional, material and affective factors that coordinate to produce a particular form of unemployment. I examined the problem of research methods in psychology and governmentality studies, particularly in relation to how to research unemployment. In order to rethink unemployment, I examined the conditions of possibility for unemployed subjectivities outside of the dominant psychological and policy explanations. In this way, I utilised a critical, 'non-disciplinary' approach to attend to the broader processes, materialities, and the daily social and research practices that (re)produce unemployment as a certain type of problem, and in doing so, also (re)produce unemployment as a certain object.

A key objective of this book was to research unemployment and unemployed subjectivity in ways that do not (re)produce 'psy-complexified' understandings of unemployment which are often taken as 'self-evident' in ES.

The 'critical' in my version of a post-disciplinary approach to unemployment is indebted to Foucault's work on 'critique'. For Foucault (2003), governmentality is related to critique. He stated that if governmentality is the "movement through which individuals are subjugated in the reality of a social practice through mechanisms of power that adhere to a truth" (p. 265), then critique is "the art of not being governed quite so much" (p. 265). Orientating my research towards critique, therefore, involves interrogating the relations of power and truth regarding 'unemployment' and the unemployed subject. Critique can provide ways through which we can destabilise how we think about 'unemployment', its 'impact' and the effects of these, including how we pose any 'solutions'. This also includes taking seriously the 'ontological politics' or thinking about the productivity of research and how it 'intervenes' in the social world (Mol, 1999). In this book, I present a bespoke attempt at deploying a post-disciplinary approach to researching unemployment that emphasises a reflexive approach to critique methods while still deploying them.

Book outline

The book has two lines of inquiry. Firstly, I argue that policy and front-line practices are constitutive factors that form unemployment. Secondly, through my research, I also demonstrate how research practices can (re)produce discourses/practices/subjects we set out to critique and rethink. The second chapter outlines a critical frame of reference that guides the book and the research. The third chapter examines psychological research on unemployment by interrogating the productivity of methods. This chapter critically reads psychology research and governmentality literature and demonstrates why critical psychologists and other critical researchers need to keep a critical lens on research practices inside and outside of the discipline. The fourth chapter provides an example of how to explore the impact of policy as representing unemployment as a particular type of problem and the implications of this political practice. In Chapter Five I discuss fieldwork in 'Active Job' which showed the nuances of affective governing by following psy-infused emotions that informed, activated and sustained dominant problematisations about unemployment. In the sixth chapter, I outline the epistemic, ethical and political implications of the research. The last chapter brings together the main arguments of the book.

A suggestion on how to use this book

This book is all about how to *do* critique through research on unemployment. Critique is an 'attitude' that shows us we are much "freer than we feel" and has the potential to transform our social world and ourselves (Foucault, 1988, p. 10). The chapters in this book provide examples of how to move forward, but they are not without problems or meant to be prescriptive. The theoretical tools were assembled to solve the issue I was (and still am) tackling. It is important here to remember that knowledge generation is political, but also partial and situated (Haraway, 1988) and is by no means exhaustive or generalisable. There are stark differences from a situated analysis in one city in Australia in the Global North, where unemployment was around 6% (at the time of the research) to other Global South countries where unemployment was and is much, much higher. Even in terms of other OECD countries with similar welfare regimes, care needs to be taken to avoid generalisations because political rationalities such as neoliberalism are "not a seamless and steely behemoth, but an evolving hybrid whose every concrete manifestation is imbued with local flavours" (Ban, 2016, p. 3).

My main arguments challenge how we think about unemployment, the work-welfare nexus, psy and the role of researchers. In places with punitive welfare regimes such as Australia, a Foucauldian-inspired bricolage that hinges on 'critique' can and should be deployed to refuse to think about unemployment as we have so far (Fryer, 2019). Even taking into account the limitations of this approach, a post-disciplinary and critical psychological perspective on unemployment is integral to challenge how the unemployed are blamed for their unemployment.

References

Abbott, T. (2015). *New jobactive service to help more jobseekers into work.* (Press release) Retrieved from https://www.pm.gov.au/media/2015-03-31/new-jobactive-services-help-more-jobseekers-work.

Abramovitz, M. (2006). Welfare reform in the United States: Gender, race and class matter. *Critical Social Policy, 26*(2), 336–364. 10.1177/0261018306062589

Australian Council of Social Services [ACOSS] (2020). *Faces of unemployment.* ACOSS.

Ban, C. (2016), *Ruling ideas: How global neoliberalism goes local.* Oxford University Press.

Baxandall, P. (2002). Explaining differences in the political meaning of unemployment across time and space. *The Journal of Socio-Economics, 31*(5), 469–502. 10.1016/S1053-5357(02)00136-1.

Blustein, D. L., Medvide, M., & Wan, C. A. (2012). A critical perspective of contemporary unemployment policy and practices. *Journal of Career Development, 29*(4), 341–356. 10.1177/0894845310397545

Coates, B., Cowgill, M., Chen, T., & Mackey, W. (2020). *Shutdown: Estimating the COVID-19 employment shock.* Grattan Institute. https://grattan.edu.au/wp-content/uploads/2020/04/Shutdown-estimating-the-COVID-19-employment-shock-Grattan-Institute.pdf

Cromby, J., & Willis, M. E. H. (2014). Nudging into subjectification: Governmentality and psychometrics. *Critical Social Policy, 34*(2), 241–259.

Drewery, W. (1998). Unemployment: What kind of problem is it? *Journal of Community & Applied Social Psychology, 8*, 101–118.

Foucault, M. (1988). Truth, power, self: An interview with Michel Foucault October 25 1982. In L. H. Martin & P. Hutton (Eds.), *Technologies of the Self: A Seminar with Michel Foucault.* University of Massachusetts Press.

Foucault, M. (2003). So it is important to think? In P. Rabinow & N. Rose (Eds.), *The Essential Foucault: Selections from Essential Works of Foucault, 1954–1984* (pp. 170–173). New York Press.

Fraser, N., & Gordon, L. (1994). A genealogy of dependency: Tracing a keyword of the US welfare state. *Signs, 19*(2), 309–336.

Friedli, L., & Stern, R. (2015). Positive affect as coercive strategy: Conditionality, activation and the role of psychology in UK government welfare programmes. *Medical Humanities, 41*, 40–47.

Fryer, D. (2012). Critical differences: The development of a community critical psychological perspective on the psychological costs of unemployment. In T. Kieselbach & S. Mannila (Eds.), *Unemployment, Precarious Work and Health: Research and Policy Issues* (pp. 473–489). Springer.

Fryer, D. (2019). Applied social psychology, the neoliberal labour-market subject and critique. In K. Doherty & D. Hodgetts (Eds.), *The SAGE Handbook of Applied Social Psychology*. SAGE.

Fryer, D., & Stambe, R. (2014a). Neo-liberal austerity and unemployment: Critical psychological issues. *The Psychologist, 27*(4), 244–248.

Fryer, D., & Stambe, R. (2014b). Work and the 'crafting of individual identities' from a critical standpoint. *The Australian Community Psychologist, 26*(1), 8–17.

Gibson, S. (2009). The effortful citizen: Discursive social psychology and welfare reform. *Journal of Community & Applied Social Psychology, 19*, 393–410.

Haraway, D. (1988). Situated knowledges: The science question in feminism and the privilege of partial perspective. *Feminist Studies, 14*(3), 575–599.

Hayne, J. (2020, May 14). Coronavirus sent shockwaves through the Australian job market. Here are the numbers you need to know. *ABC News*. https://www.abc.net.au/news/2020-05-14/coronavirus-job-figures-numbers-released/12248280

International Labour Organisation [ILO] (2020). *COVID and the world of work: Fifth Edition*, 30 June. Available at https://www.ilo.org/wcmsp5/groups/public/@dgreports/@dcomm/documents/briefingnote/wcms_749399.pdf

Kesley-Sugg, A., & Tickle, M. (2020, May 11). Lost your job because of coronavirus? You might face an identity crisis – but you can overcome it. *ABC News*. https://www.abc.net.au/news/2020-05-11/coronavirus-sudden-unemployment-and-impact-on-identity/12206868

Klein, E. (2020). Australia has been stigmatising unemployed people for almost 100 years. COVID-19 is our big chance to change this. *The Conversation*. https://theconversation.com/australia-has-been-stigmatising-unemployed-people-for-almost-100-years-covid-19-is-our-big-chance-to-change-this-143349

Mol, A. (1999). Ontological politics: A word and some questions. In J. Law & J. Hassard (Eds.), *Actor Network Theory and After*. Oxford.

Moreira, A., & Lødemel I. (2014). Chapter 11. Governing activation in the 21st century. In I. Lødemel & A. Moreira (Eds.), *Activation or Workfare?: Governance and Neo-liberal Convergence* (International Policy Exchange Series). Oxford University Press.

Nolan, D. (2003). The constitution of unemployment: Journalism as a technology of citizenship. *Southern Review, 36.3*(2003), 64–81.

Office of the Prime Minister [OPM]. (2020, April 23). Press conference. Australian Government. https://www.pm.gov.au/media/press-conference-australian-parliament-house-act-23april

Parker, I. (1997). Psychology, subjectivity and resistance. *Forum Kritische Psycholgie, 38*, 136–145.

Pultz, S. (2018). Shame and passion: The affective governing of young unemployed people. *Theory & Psychology*, Advanced online publication retrieved from http://journals.sagepub.com/doi/pdf/10.1177/0959354318759608.

Rose, N. (1996). *Inventing ourselves: Psychology, power and personhood*. Cambridge University Press.

Stambe, R., & Fryer, D. (2015). How the unemployed disappear and why it matters. *The Conversation*. Retrieved from http://theconversation.com/how-the-unemployed-disappear-and-why-it-matters-35850

Statistics South Africa. (2020). Statistical release, quarterly Labour force survey quarter 1: 2020. http://www.statssa.gov.za/publications/P0211/P02111stQuarter2020.pdf

Walkerdine, V., & Bansel, P. (2010). Neoliberalism, work and subjectivity: Towards a more complex account. *SAGE Handbook of Identities* (pp. 492–507). SAGE.

Walters, W. (2000). *Unemployment and government: Genealogies of the social*. Cambridge University Press.

Ware, F., Breheny, M., & Forster, M. (2017). The politics of government 'support' in Aotearoa/New Zealand: Reinforcing and reproducing the poor citizenship of young Māori parents. *Critical Social Policy*, *37*(4), 499–519. 10.1177/0261018316672111

Watts, R. (2016). Running on empty: Australia's neoliberal social security system, 1988–2015. In J. Mays, G. Marston, & J. Tomlinson (Eds.), *Basic Income in Australia and New Zealand: Perspectives from the Neoliberal Frontier*. Palgrave Macmillian.

Wright, S., Fletcher, D. R., & Stewart, A. B. R. (2020). Punitive benefit sanctions, welfare conditionality, and the social abuse of unemployed people in Britain: Transforming claimants into offenders? *Social Policy & Administration*, *54*(2), 278–294.

Yang, J. (2015). *Unknotting the heart: Unemployment and therapeutic governance in China*. Cornell University Press.

2

PUTTING CRITIQUE TO WORK

Introduction

The second chapter will outline a 'post-disciplinary' approach to researching unemployment that is underpinned by Foucault's work on 'critique'. This approach removes the humanist preoccupation with the rational/unitary subject, essentialism and modernist fixation with progress that often characterises psychological research. The challenge for critical researchers is avoiding uncritical research practices. Conversely, it is also easy to get bogged down in methodolatry such that we lose sight of the criticalness of our research and the political implication of knowledge production (Chamberlain, 2000). For critical psychology, a key risk to mitigate is reinscribing the psy-complex, and with it, problematic notions of the self, the world, progress and knowledge production.

I suggest following Jackson and Mazzei (2012) by returning to first principles. These authors discuss the practice of 'plugging in' as a way of "thinking methodologically" (p. 261) by thinking *with* theory. Plugging in is a way to put theory 'to work', to produce knowledge as an ongoing assemblage that establishes connections between "a field of reality (the world) and a field of representation (the book) and a field of subjectivity (the author)" (p. 263). The assemblage also destabilises knowledge as a 'final arrival' and instead something moving and unfinished. Just as objects, subjects and the constituting apparatuses are unfixed and changing. 'Thinking methodologically' also involves acknowledging how methods, as epistemically informed practices, may not automatically cohere methodologically with our broader project. According to Jackson and Mazzei, their interviews, were "failed from the start" (p. 264), and I would add that qualitative research methods more broadly may also be 'failed from the start'. The authors' solution was to 'plug into' machines, that is, "theories, data, methods, becomings" (p. 263) to do 'something else'. For my research, this 'something else'

DOI: 10.4324/9781003112518-2

is the refusal to produce 'evidence' about the 'psychological consequences' of 'unemployment'.

Below, I 'plug-in' to a frame-of-reference that is Foucauldian-inspired and non-disciplinary. I will outline the theoretical tools that the book will draw upon, all of which help to situate unemployment as an active concept, being remade through policy, legislation, front-line organisations and research. I present a research design to rethink how we produce knowledge about the unemployed and how best to 'help' them.

A critical frame-of-reference: Critique, 'truth', methods

Social science research is situated within a frame-of-reference. A 'frame of reference' refers to an interrelated set of philosophical assumptions about epistemology; ontology; how knowledge claims are constructed and legitimised; how knowledge functions societally and how we position the 'subject' (Stambe & Fryer, 2014). Although dividing research into different categories depending on a frame-of-reference is itself a modernist practice (Brinkmann, 2014), I find it useful to examine the difficulties of doing poststructural research with traditional qualitative research methods becuase the frame-of-reference of the research and methodology will each have implications for the other. Although 'methodology' and 'method' are sometimes used interchangeably, I prefer to separate them to help unpack research practices. I define 'methodology' as the theory of method (method + logos) where 'method' refers to the techniques used to generate 'data'. I do not imply that method (action) is distinct from methodology (theory) but I will engage in an academic exercise to make explicit the machinations and veridiction of method (that includes methodology and ethics), which is always present but not necessarily discussed. I will outline the frame-of-reference in the following paragraphs before explicating in more detail the usefulness of Foucault's work.

The 'critical frame-of-reference' for my research consists of four interrelated axes. These axes form the parameters of my research design and, as a result, constitute the (meta)theoretical position of the research. Firstly, the research is a means of critique in a Foucauldian sense – refusing to be governed in specific ways. Secondly, the research aims to challenge psychological knowledges and practices insofar as they reproduce a particular 'unemployed subject'. A part of analysing the psy-complex also implies positioning the ontological and epistemological foundations of psychological knowledges and practices (Teo, 2009) as a discipline to be critiqued. Rimke (2016, p. 7) summarises these foundations into ten characteristics. The characteristics which are relevant to this discussion include suspending: the tendency to reduce the complexity of the social world to causal explanations, particularly about the individual; essentialising and naturalising human beings as stable, unitary, rational entities; and positivism. The third axis rejects modernist principles of truth-work including making predictions, providing solutions, gathering 'evidence' for social ordering and contributing to a broader sense of societal progress (Bacchi & Goodwin, 2016).

The last element of the frame-of-reference refers to a different way of approaching 'truth' and this concern, along with the practice of 'critique', is crucial to the aims of this book. Following Foucault (2002), I see 'truth' as a verb rather than a noun (hence I use terms such as 'truthing'). The ontological and epistemological foundations of disciplinary knowledges and practices are positioned as 'regimes of truth' to be critiqued. These 'regimes of truth' relate to discourse or the "body of anonymous, historical rules, always determined in the time and space that have defined a given period, and for a given social, economic, geographical, or linguistic area, the conditions of the operation of the enunciative function" (Foucault, p. 131). These historical rules are not rules in the strictest sense (Cousins & Hussain, 1984) but rather form a "complex group of relations that function as a rule" (Foucault, p. 74). Discourse surpasses the symbolic-material boundary since, "in a discourse, words, materialities and practices hang together in a specific, historically and culturally situated way" (Mol, 2008, p. 8). Discourse sets the boundaries around its domain, and with visibility and authority, certain things are possible to say, and alternative possibilities are closed down. In this way, discourse establishes what it is "possible to say within the true" (Bacchi & Bonham, 2014, p. 179) or that which enables "speakers to be taken seriously" (Dreyfus & Rabinow, 1983, p. 48). Discourses are multiple, multi-level and sometimes contradictory (Bacchi & Goodwin, 2016). Research is one way of manufacturing 'truth' and is a complex set of discursive practices within a regime of truth. In sum, this critical frame-of-reference is heavily influenced by a Foucauldian-inspired poststructural perspective. In the following section, I will elaborate more on deploying such a perspective to rethink unemployment and the unemployed.

The usefulness of Foucauldian-inspired poststructuralism

Some researchers claim that any attempt to make sense of 'unemployment' that in effect separates the social and the individual will be "inadequate for encapsulating the complexities surrounding its meaning and impact" (Cullen & Hodgetts, 2001, p. 34). While I do want to have a conversation about 'unemployment' that rejoins the social and the subject, I am also aware that reinserting the subject back into the social can ascribe to the person-in-context position (Nic Giolla Easpaig et al., 2014). As Nic Giolla Easpaig et al. point out, theorising subjectivity through the person-in-context framework reiterates the agency/structure binary by positioning the individual as an agent who interacts and negotiates through different levels of their social environment and can imply a one-way interaction. For this reason, I am interested in exploring the *complexity* of what it is to be unemployed in Australia. Specifically, this exploration enables me to do the following: reject the modernist individual, explore the selves we can/not be through specific apparatuses of subjectification; take the distress of unemployment seriously; as well as examine and contest the (re)production of oppressive discourses. Oppressive discourses refer to "the disadvantage and injustice some people suffer ... because of the everyday practices of a well-intentioned society" (Young, 1988, p. 272).

Consequently, I take a Foucauldian-inspired poststructuralist perspective that focuses on the (re)constitution of subjectivity.

Subjectification refers here to "how inner processes are reshaped amid economic and political reforms, violence and social suffering" (Biehl et al., 2007, p. 1). Subjectification is both being a subject and the constitution of the subject through power relations (Butler, 1997). This double-meaning avoids the agency/structure dichotomy where discussions are caught between a subject who is socialised through different ideologies and social structures and the voluntarist subject who is able to make choices of their free will. In this way, I also aim to avoid the pre-discursive subject, one who is influenced by the social world but nevertheless, exists prior to and outside the world, and who is able to make meaning about their experiences. I still draw on the importance of the person-in-the-world but instead of the person existing prior to an act (the 'I' that does things) a person is constituted as a subject through the act (Butler, 1990). I use 'constitution' because it captures the idea of the subjected being 'brought into existence' but also of 'taking up' where the "taker and the taken are, in a sense, 'the same' mutually determining" (Jones, 1997 p. 267). Subjection occurs in the discursive possibilities for being, and that at the "convergence of such discursive injunctions", there is a potential for a "complex reconfiguration" (Butler, 1990, p. 145). In other words, the agentic potential for the subject is possible through the discourses available thus "there is only the taking up of the tools where they lie, where the very 'taking up' is enabled by the tool lying there" (p. 145).

Foucault's work on subjectivity is useful in research that is interested in critiquing (rather than reproducing) the psy-complex since Foucault took an explicit anti-psychological stance on subjectivity (Valverde, 2004). Instead of mapping a static self according to generalisations about normal human characteristics and capabilities (which can then be accurately measured with a personality test and so forth), the focus is on the ongoing constitution of a person. By 'ongoing' I am referring to how a "human being is in flux, in process at every moment being disciplined, regulated, normalised, produced, and at the same time, resisting, shifting, changing, producing" (St Pierre, 2011a, p. 46). Our subjectivity is precarious, constantly changing through discourse, which means we are not stuck in a pre-determined state.

Significantly, what it is to be 'human' from a Foucauldian-inspired perspective is intimately entangled in the social world. We cannot talk about what is inside the heads of people without joining 'macro' and 'micro' politics together in the conversation. Understanding the subject in such a way helps to resist reducing the complexity of the social world, including ourselves, into individual-society dualism (Henriques et al., 1984). It also helps to circumvent the priority of the cognitive 'I' constituted through the psy-complex and the potential for rethinking psy-complexified practices and the individualist-therapeutic state (McNamee, 2015). Unemployment within this frame-of-reference must be something more than the attitudes, faulty cognitions and negative affects of the (individual) unemployed. The point of inquiry, therefore, shifts to understanding the constitutive effects of socio-historical, material, affective and contextual factors.

Subjectivity and unemployment

To understand how 'unemployment' and subjectivity are intertwined, I find a useful starting point to return to Foucault's (2008) first lecture from *The Birth of Biopolitics*. In these lectures, Foucault makes it clear he is not interested in how an object (such as 'unemployment') was discovered or conversely how it is proven not to exist. It is irrelevant whether unemployment is a 'real thing' or an economic construction for example. The key point is to examine how an object *does exist* so far as "it is precisely a set of practices, real practices, which established it and thus imperiously marks it out in reality" (p. 19). A task of my research is, therefore, to unpack the interconnections between a whole set of practices that adhere to truth, which turn 'unemployment' into an object.

By 'practices' Foucault was referring to the "places" where what can be said and done, discourses, and strategies "meet and interconnect" (Foucault, 1991, p. 75). There is a judicial component (the rules given) and a veridicition component (the reasons given according to discourses of true/false) (Flynn, 2005). Kendall (2011) describes how Foucault's work on the self was more concerned with how institutions and systems have been invented to problematise the self. Consequently, I propose that a focus on how the unemployed self is problematised within ES and psychological literature is a means for locating this 'marking out' in part through the practices that (re)subjectify the unemployed subject.

My research studied the practices of this (re)subjectification within the domain of ES in Australia. ES problematises 'unemployment' at the level of the individual (Dean, 1995). This is consistent with the political rationality of 'neoliberalism' as defined by Foucault (2008). Political rationalities are "a way of doing things that was oriented to specific objectives and that reflected on itself in characteristic ways" (Rose et al., 2006, p. 84). In this context, state intervention is not directed towards regulation of the labour market but rather through intervention through society "in its fabric and depth" (p. 145). Within welfare policy in Australia, neoliberal intervention includes the responsibilisation of the individual to (re)gain employment.

Governing the unemployed

Some researchers have drawn on Foucault's understanding of 'governmentality' to analyse the logic and practices of ES and subjectification. Government, for Foucault, was not just the representation of the state or political structures but also was the means of regulating behaviour towards certain ends (Dean, 2010). Governmentality refers to rationality and practices, drawing upon expertise, which aims to improve a population (Foucault, 2003a). Dean (1995) clarified that this central problem of governing, the "conduct of conduct" (Foucault, 2003c, p. 138), suggests two forms of the constitution of the self. In the first instance, the 'conduct of conduct' refers to how authorities seek to shape people's behaviours, thoughts, aspirations and capacities through various strategies driven towards satisfaction of certain goals. In Australia, the governing of the unemployed is through processes of activation to produce the ideal unemployed subject, the 'job seeker' ('clients').

The second meaning refers to how people self-problematise and self-regulate through technologies of the self (Foucault, 2003c) to change themselves into the desired subjects. In ES, this self-governmentality manifests through wanting to work upon oneself and actively engage in programs of reformation to improve job readiness. The governmentality framework enables an analysis of the multiple strategies deployed by different authorities to govern so people act in desired ways (Rose, 1996). Therefore, governmentality can be understood as the "movement through which individuals are subjugated in the reality of a social practice through mechanisms of power that adhere to a truth" (Foucault, 2003a, p. 266).

Governmentality is thus used to study how different knowledges, attached to various authorities, inform practices and technologies that are developed to guide people's voluntary behaviour. The concept is particularly useful for examining neoliberal political rationalities that utilise 'freedom' and 'free choice' to produce subjectivities that are self-optimising and entrepreneurial (Foucault, 2008). At the same time, these subjectivities are taken-for-granted practices, knowledges and assumptions are interrogated and dismantled. As Dean (2010) argued, governmentality and critique make it possible for us to take on an "experimental attitude where we can test the limits of our governmental rationalities [and] the forms of power and domination they involve" (p. 35). The practices can no longer be presented as self-evident or inevitable, and we can "think in different ways about the action on the actions of the self and others" (p. 36). By eschewing the idea that power is traceable back to a single source and instead focusing on politics as 'governing at a distance', a governmentality approach enables critique to go beyond structure/agency, public/private, and other limiting dichotomies.

Governmentality provides an analytical lens for how new markets and expertise are enabled within a governing complex. In Australia, both the 'informal' and 'formal' psychologisation of unemployment are present. Some provider organisations develop psy-informed 'activation' training programs in-house while others purchase programs from third parties. For example, psychologists act as contractors to provide psychologised services to individual clients, to assist the employment consultants to develop 'skills' relating to motivating the unemployed and/or improve clients' 'attitudes'. Esher House (n.d.) is one such organisation that incorporates behavioural strategies informed by Positive Psychology to develop assessment and training programs to improve outcomes for Government policy objectives. While some research suggests programs based on Positive Psychology improve subjective wellbeing (Dambrun & Dubuy, 2014), there is conflicting evidence about whether psychological interventions improve job outcomes (Koopman et al., 2017; Liu et al., 2014). However, my arguments in this book are not concerned with whether these 'solutions' work but the implications for how unemployment is understood and how this mobilises an unemployed subject. Specifically, these psy knowledges inform, sustain, complicate, activate or may even disrupt the power-knowledge in ES in Australia. I consider 'psy' discourses to be crucial in understand the meaning what it is to be unemployed.

The role of the psy-complex and 'affect/emotions' to govern the unemployed

Practices of governing others and self-governing rely on psy-complexified discourses and power-knowledges within welfare organisations in Australia. Although governmentality research in Australia does not discuss the psy-complex directly, this body of literature has captured how clients are required to undergo counselling and training to 'improve' job readiness, motivation, self-esteem and confidence. Furthermore, civil society actors are conscripted to govern by enabling such actors to embrace psy-complexified notions of the self (Dean, 1995). Hook (2010) argued that governmentality extends to how psychological technologies of affect are involved in the (re)subjectification process. As Bjerg and Staunæs (2011) state, "affects and affectivity are not simply by-products or something to be overcome, but the core matter to be managed by and through" (p. 138). I view affects as relational, an affective circulation that is embedded in situated practices and connected to subjects' embodied capacity to affect and be affected (Wetherell, 2012). How discourses of affect are involved with re-subjectification corresponds with the Foucauldian notion of power-knowledge and psychologised knowledges/practices of the self, the potential self, and the way we can talk about and experience emotions (McAvoy, 2015).

Affect, as an intensity, is distinguishable from 'emotions' but not mutually exclusive. I see emotions as the cultural and historical component of 'affect', that come to the fore when we try to understand and discuss 'affect' (see Reddy, 2001). Hence 'emotions' are discursive practices or an 'emotional regime'. By this I mean the normative style of emotional management, part of 'common sense', that is situated, historical and political (Reddy, 2001). In this context, the focus should be on how practices are "clumped, who gets to do what, when and what relations do an affective practice make, enact, disrupt, and reinforce" (Wetherell, 2012, p. 17).

I agree with Walker et al. (2014) that studying 'affect/emotions/feelings' is a way to take peoples' distress seriously without having to (re)inscribe psychologised notions of 'health' or 'disorder'. Instead, research can focus on how 'emotions' or affect is used to manage the unemployed to facilitate compliance. By focusing on the use of emotions and what these discursive practices do, I can attend to how governing is legitimated and deployed via certain technologies, strategies and authorities and how psychology is part of this assemblage. Indeed, the psychologised notions of 'emotions' with the associated technologies, assessments and practices of reformation are connected to the 'regime of truth' about emotions. Psy knowledges are part of the 'emotional regime'. As argued by Rose (1996) the psychological sciences, its history and current use, present normative management strategies to contain or mobilise emotions. This 'expertise' merges a technical rationality with the 'truth' about individuals that are problematised psychologically.

According to McDonald and Marston (2005), employment consultants in previous iterations of ES relied on psychologised knowledge claims to diffuse anger and manage clients. Furthermore, Dassinger (2013) describes forms of governing used to reform the subjectivities of the unemployed through training and counselling were affects/emotions such as 'shame' are utilised in processes of (re)subjectification to induce self-responsibility. Employment consultants are likely to take up these knowledges to manage communicative processes and relations with clients. This includes the practices of knowing, problematising and working on the self so workers can manage their emotions. The object of this affective self-governing is to regulate the affective dimension of ES to deploy emotions to manage clients (Penz et al., 2017). I contribute to this body of literature by taking a critical psychological lens and unsettling some of the 'self-evident' uses of affect and emotion in the sociology of emotion literature generally (Wetherell, 2012) and focus the research lens on how affective governmentality and psy-complexified practices function in ES.

The strategies deployed by employment consultants to govern the unemployed, and how these are (re)shaped by contractual obligations, organisational procedures and priorities, and material circumstances provide a rich landscape for researching the psychologisation of unemployment. Researchers have looked at how the materials used by employment consultants shape how the unemployed are encouraged to take up certain understandings of the self. Cromby and Willis (2014) unpack the positive psychology VIA questionnaire that encouraged clients to see themselves through a 'strengths' lens. The researchers argue that the psychometric qualities of the VIA are questionable but even so, they highlight how the psychologised knowledges that inform and authorise the tool are part of the 'nudging' strategies within the UK welfare state apparatus. Additionally, psychological intervention to improve 'positive affect' while also implicated in punitive and coercive practices of 'workfare' (UK context) can also silence voices of critique within ES (Friedli & Stern, 2015). Indeed, these authors note psychological knowledges used in the "monitoring, modifying and punishing" (p. 42) of clients are seldom criticised.

Bringing a critical psychological approach to the Australian welfare context blends a governmentality approach with a critical lens to also examine the psy-complex and methodology. I focus on how various elements that are historical and culturally contingent are coordinated and (re)assembled to strategically solve 'problems'. Research methods are not separate from these 'apparatuses' and so are not 'describing' subjectivity but are part of the system of discursive and governing practices that contribute to the conditions of possibilities for how unemployment is experienced. While governmentality is not a novel approach to thinking about unemployment in Australia, my book presents a different way to research front-line organisations by focusing on the practices that make and remake the unemployed and workers in ambiguous, political, contested and affective spaces while keeping research methods within the critical lens.

Implications for critical methodology

The critical frame-of-reference explicated above has implications for methodology and method. Any methodology and method chosen need to accomplish the following: challenge taken-for-granted assumptions about 'unemployment' and the 'unemployed' (critique); resist (and not reproduce) the psy-complex and the associated epistemological and ontological assumptions, and finally; take an anti-modernist stance on the 'subject', knowledge generation and the function of knowledge.

In Foucauldian-like inquiries, the researcher's role is to untangle 'lines of force' (power) and 'lines of enunciation' (knowledge) (Deleuze, 1992) to map the "dispositions, manoeuvres, tactics, techniques and functionings" (Foucault, 1991, p. 26). The point is to demonstrate the materiality of knowledge and its effects on the constitution of objects and subjects. By showing the contingency of knowledge, research can point to how certain regimes of 'knowledge' come to dominate and other ways of 'knowing' are dismissed or disappeared. Research, as a practice of 'critique', should open up the spaces to challenge dominant knowledges and practices so that repeating or reproducing these discourses/practices becomes a hard thing to do (Foucault, 2003b).

Foucauldian-inspired poststructuralist research understood within a critical frame-of-reference is inherently political. Here 'political' refers to the strategic relations which act upon lives (Bacchi, 2012). For example, researchers completing Foucauldian-like research engage with a multitude of methodologies and associated methods for political ends. Research is also political, even if it does not have explicit political intentions. Returning to the idea of power-knowledge, the production of knowledge is political insofar as research not only influences other practices (other research, theory building, policy development and so on) but it is interventionist. To explain this point further, I find it useful to draw on Mol's (1999, pp. 74–75) 'ontological politics' (especially Bacchi's, 2012, use of the concept). Mol defines ontology as the 'real' or the "conditions of possibility we live with". Because "reality does not precede the mundane practices in which we interact ... but is rather shaped within these practices", then reality is political since it is crafted, open and contest(ed)able. Research methods can be seen as intervening in the world because "methods, their rules, and even more method's practices, not only describe but also help to produce our world" (Law, 2004, p. 5).

Repositioning research practices as an intervention into the world highlights an 'action' element of all research and raises important questions when using as a Foucauldian-inspired critical frame-of-reference. Not only does the research challenge self-evident renditions of 'unemployment' and the 'psychologisation of the unemployed', but research methods are also under question. Methods, as epistemically informed practices, also have taken-for-granted assumptions which may be contradictory to the broader frame-of-reference. Research methods operate through 'regimes of truth' that continue circulations of truths about objects.

Such 'regimes' are present in every society and discipline that set the criteria for what is to be considered 'knowledge'. Additionally, these regimes of truth are driven by a 'will' or pursuit of knowledge, and these discourses are deeply contentious and contested. The focus should be on the rules, how the 'truth' and the 'false' are separated, how such separation is controversial and alternatives are presented, and the implicated power relations, attached to the true, that produce certain subjects and spaces (Foucault, 1980, p. 131).

These regimes involve 'games' of truth where the emphasis is on the rules which produce 'truth', what can be considered valid, or what is sidelined as 'false' (Foucault, 2003d, p. 38). These games of truth are connected to the self, since "the games of truth and error through which being [is] historically constituted as experience" (Foucault, 1985, pp. 6–7) or how experience can be thought and discussed as such. Rabinow and Rose (2003) suggested that the best way to analyse these games is through technologies or "the intellectual and practical instruments and devices enjoined upon human beings to shape and guide their ways of 'being human'" (p. xxi). Interviews or observations in a research setting can also be understood as technologies.

Research methods and the disciplines within which the research is situated operate through the 'regimes of truth' that continue circulations of truths about objects (which are then constituted by the practices that allow these objects to be known). In other words, it is the knowledge-making practices embedded in research methods that critical research is trying to untangle. This is important to research that aims to question the psy-complex. In extending the focus of critique to method and the psy-complex, I am in agreement with Parker (2005) that "the most important battleground now is methodology … what has held psychology together and defined it as a distinct discipline is its method, the way it goes about knowing those that it observes and regulates" (p. 1). As Parker suggested, how psy-complexifiers claim to know things is so important that critique should "emphasise the activity or process of research rather than the objects" which are allegedly known in dominant psy-complex discourse (p. 3). Parker elaborated on this assertion within a Foucauldian frame-of-reference, which he positions as having "profound implications for methodology" (p. 3). He asserted that the production of knowledge is more important than what is uncovered because "different disciplines (such as psychology) operate as 'regimes of truth' in which there is a circulation of knowledge about objects that are *formed by the very practices through which they are known*" (p. 3, my emphasis). The way that we do our research needs to be attended to when we discuss our research. The knowledge produced through research understood within the power-knowledge nexus renders method and research practices in need of critique.

Researching governing practices: A research strategy

The case study used in this book draws on a quasi-ethnographic study conducted in one ES provider in an urban centre in South East Queensland. I will call this provider 'Active Job'. The study explored how power was embedded in the mundane practices of activation. The quasi-ethnographic research included in-depth qualitative interviews, participant observations, document and policy analysis. The fieldwork was completed between October 2015 and August 2016 across four sites (North-1, North-2, West, South). Participant observations provided a lens to understand additional dimensions of the everyday work practices within Active Job and varied from 2 hours to a full working day. Observations included observing the group case management, informal interviews with workers about incidents that had occurred during their day and team meetings.

Interviews were conducted with employment consultants (n = 13), four of whom were male, and the remainder were female. Participants' ages ranged from the early 20s to early 60s. Five participants agreed to be interviewed more than once to answer questions that arose during the course of observations. There are 26 recorded interviews in total. Twelve participants had worked in ES before the introduction of *jobactive*. Interviews focused on the workers' daily routines and in particular, the changes to their daily practices via the new service delivery model. I utilised Rose's (1999a) dimensions of governmentality, Bonham and Bacchi's (2017) poststructural interview analysis, and *What's the problem represented to be an approach* to guide analysis of policy and documents (Bacchi & Goodwin, 2016) alongside a close reading of Foucauldian and post-Foucauldian texts. I explain these research processes in more detail elsewhere (see Stambe, 2020, pp. 97–118). Nevertheless, I also come back to some key components of these processes as they are relevant in upcoming chapters.

What I want to emphasise here is the methodological work done to justify methods. To reshape the research so that it coheres with the theoretical concepts described in the front section of this chapter, I used Foucault's tools, the apparatus and problematisation, and the 'ethnographic imagination' to 'think with theory' and "do something else" (Jackson & Mazzei, 2012, p. 262).

Thinking with the apparatus and the ethnographic imagination

My primary focus in this research is to explore how a person can experience unemployement via the reconstitution processes of a multitude of intersecting power relations, knowledge claims, discourses, technologies, institutions and practices. To this end, I use the apparatus as a guiding methodological framework. The apparatus is a system of relations that emerges from a specific historical problem. The apparatus targets a section of society to define, constitute and regulate through power-knowledge. It is assembled to resolve an "urgent need" and "thus has a dominant strategic function" (Foucault, 1980, p. 195). It is through the apparatus, power-knowledge, principles and agendas of governing are applied.

To explore the apparatus and how 'unemployment' is marked out in reality through the (re)subjectification of the unemployed I consider how the *jobactive* employment model is constructed. As a way in, I position *jobactive* ontologically as an apparatus. The *jobactive* apparatus makes visible the 'unemployed' by marking out the population through an assemblage of practices and knowledge claims about what 'unemployment' is and how 'unemployment' is a problem that needs to be resolved by the *jobactive* apparatus. The *jobactive* apparatus draws together specific strategies and technologies of intervention through administrative procedures and frameworks for providers to operate, form service delivery models and incorporate a variety of institutions for implementation of the models, while also creating scope for philanthropy. The *jobactive* apparatus coordinates certain discourses about 'unemployment' and similarly silences subjugated discourses. However, it should also be noted that the 'apparatus' is more complex than simply performing an uncontested and uniform machine-like function. Despite the strategic function of the apparatus, there are unplanned effects and although stable, the apparatus is not static (Rabinow & Rose, 2003). *Jobactive* is the latest iteration of ES and represents the *current* formation of the apparatus that governs the unemployed. I outline two ways the case study in this book researches the jobactive apparatus.

Firstly, Governmentality produces a series of strategies for the 'conduct of conduct' in order to address whatever is deemed to be a problem (or, more accurately within this frame of reference, constituted as being a problem) that these strategies aim to address (Teghtsoonian, 2016). My research explores the 'problem' that the *jobactive* apparatus is assembled to 'resolve'. As a 'top-down' approach, this part of the book will focus on the problem of unemployment as produced through research and the governmental practices that occur through documents, policies, administrative procedures and the like but also what is happening 'on the ground'. This includes thinking through how psychological 'expertise' helps to constitute problems within various institutions "in a way amenable to 'subjectification', so that psychology and psychologists would be able to provide solutions" (Rose, 1996, p. 84). The way that the experience of 'unemployment' has been made meaningful through psychologised discourses (Fryer & Stambe, 2014; Fryer et al., 2020) here provides a way for analysing the psychologised knowledges and practices that occur on the ground.

Secondly, I use an 'ethnographic imagination' as a way of 'thinking ethnographically' to link together the routines, practices, governing strategies, problems, the constitution of spaces and subjects, technologies, authorities and discursive practices of the *jobactive* apparatus. An 'ethnographic imagination' is not an ethnography in the more traditional anthropological sense (see Atkinson, 2015) and so I also use the term 'quasi-ethnography'. Instead, this set of research practices draws upon the 'spirit' of ethnography as a 'way of seeing' the "beliefs, the values, the material conditions *and* structural forces that underwrite the socially patterned behaviours" (Forsey, 2010, p. 567). Brady (2014) refashioned this idea of the 'ethnographic imagination' as a sensitisation to the "concrete practices within a milieu" (p. 4). As Brady and Lippert (2016) explained, this sensitivity focuses on the situated context wherein problematisation, subjectivity or governance strategies are assembled through the accounts provided by "situated actors" (p. 271). This literature follows a reading of Foucault's later work in which he moved away from exploring the power-knowledge nexus (and discourse as a self-referencing system), and focused on 'thought' and individual 'thinkers' as they problematise rationalities of a particular time and place (Collier, 2009). They assert that interviewing provides an ethnographic account of the governing strategies and 'problems' that may not have been uncovered by focusing just on the archive (Brady 2014).

I utilise this imagination to trace 'problems' in my research practices and 'sensitise' or sharpen my focus during fieldwork and in the analysis. I made some major departures on issues relating to interviewing and the subject, which I discuss in later chapters. Following the 'problems' that are present in the research field (under *jobactive*) and the discussions with workers provided a way to examine 'thought' (knowledge) as it manifests in the research situation. The focus in this section is to unpack how "thought is not what inhabits a certain conduct and gives it meaning; rather, it is what allows one to step back from this way of acting or to react, to present it to oneself as an object of thought and to question it as to its meaning, its conditions, and its goals" (Foucault, 2003e, p. 23). I find it useful to deploy problematisation as a way to uncover how an issue, object or cohort are established as a particular kind of problem, which then renders them amenable to thought (Foucault, 1985).

Focusing on problems also encourages researchers to attend to the mundane, the struggles, tensions and negotiations that may slightly change thinking or illuminate the unexpected (Rose, 1999b). Problems are identifiable through policy, legislation, and research. My own research further uncovers that problems are identifiable through the design of office space, the overall strategy of activation, the service delivery model, the problems of daily work enunciated by workers (and the techniques invented to 'solve' these problems), the authorities called upon to justify measures, the subjects produced, and the overall objective of strategies employed.

By centring analysis on the technologies, discourses and actual practices of governing, I locate the frictions and difficulties of policy/program implementation and locate the intended and unintended effects that nuance the constitution of subjects in ES. As Foucault (1991) mentioned when he was studying the Bentham prison, the actual practices of the everyday functioning of the prison were "a witches' brew compared to the beautiful Benthamite machine" (p. 81). Examining practices of governing also requires a keen eye for catching the contradictions, misadventures or failures of governing (Li, 2003). The workers' ability to enact policy, or use discretion to resist or rework these practices, is governed by organisational procedures and priorities and the possibility for using discretionary practices is contingent on the governing of the employment consultants as workers (van Berkel, 2013). The practices of 'governing at a distance' and 'at close range' overlap (Carter, 2018) in these spaces where institutional, policy, legislative and vocational concerns converge. The office floors of *jobactive* can be seen as "a thickly layered texture of political struggles concerning power and authority, cultural negotiations over identity and social constructions of the problem at hand" (Forrester 1992, p. 47). The apparatus and ethnographic imagination helped to trace practices of power-knowledge and resistance to uncover subjectivity as the site upon which governance is enacted and the materiality of politics. Using research to make visible the apparatus of interconnections, and the broader social terrain from which they emerged, can unsettle taken-for-granted assumptions about unemployment. The additional challenge pursued in this book is how to do this work of tracing the constituent features of *jobactive*, while also holding the same critical lens over the research practices.

Concluding Comments

In this chapter, I have outlined a Foucauldian-inspired, non-disciplinary toolbox to 'think with theory' and apply Foucault's critique through research practices. This chapter highlighted how unemployment is seen as an active concept, being remade through policy, legislation, front-line organisations *and* research. The rest of this book will demonstrate how to uncover the conditions that make certain renditions of unemployment possible. This book will highlight the importance of considering the productive space between critical theory and fieldwork and its value to *a* 'post-disciplinary' approach committed to challenging social inequalities and refusing the fixed identities offered to the unemployed.

References

Atkinson, P. (2015). *For ethnography*. SAGE.

Bacchi, C. (2012). Strategic interventions and ontological politics: Research as political practice. In A. Bletsas & C. Beasley's (Eds.), *Engaging with Carol Bacchi: Strategic Interventions with Exchanges*. University of Adelaide Press.

Bacchi, C., & Bonham, J. (2014). Reclaiming discursive practices as an analytic focus: Political implications. *Foucault Studies,* 17 173–192.

Bacchi, C., & Goodwin, S. (2016). *Poststructural policy analysis: A guide to practice.* Springer.

Biehl, J., Good, B., & Kleinman, A. (2007). *Subjectivity: Ethnographic investigations.* University of California Press.

Bjerg, H., & Staunæs, D. (2011). Self-management through shame: Uniting governmentality studies and the 'affective turn'. *Ephemera: Theory & Politics in Organizations, 11*(2), 138–156.

Bonham, J., & Bacchi, C. (2017). Cycling 'subjects' in *ongoing-formation*: The politics of interviews and interview analysis. *Journal of Sociology, 53*(3), 687–703. 10.1177/1440783317715805

Brady, M. (2014). Ethnographies of neoliberal governmentalities: From the neoliberal apparatus to neoliberalism and governmental assemblages. *Foucault Studies, 18*, 11–33. 10.22439/fs.v0i18.4649

Brady, M., & Lippert, R. K. (2016). Governmentalities, the ethnographic imaginary, and beyond. In M. Brady & R. K. Lippert (Eds.), *Governing Practices: Neoliberalism, Governmentality and the Ethnographic Imaginary*. University of Toronto Press.

Brinkmann, S. (2014). Doing without data. *Qualitative Inquiry, 20*(6), 720–725.

Butler, J. (1990). *Gender trouble: Feminism and the subversion of identity*. Routledge.

Butler, J. (1997). *The psychic life of power: Theories in subjection*. Standford University Press.

Carter, P. (2018). Governing spaces: A multi-sited ethnography of governing welfare reform at close range and at a distance. *Critical Policy Studies*, 1–21. 10.1080/19460171.2016.1208109

Chamberlain, K. (2000). Methodolatry and qualitative health research. *Journal of Health Psychology, 5*(3), 285–296. 10.1177/135910530000500306

Collier, S. (2009). Topologies of power: Foucault's analysis of political government beyond 'governmentality'. *Theory, Culture & Society, 26*(6), 78–108. 10.1177/0263276409347694

Cousins, M., & Hussain, A. (1984). *Michel Foucault*. Palgrave Macmillan.

Cromby, J., & Willis, M. E. H. (2014). Nudging into subjectification: Governmentality and psychometrics. *Critical Social Policy, 34*(2), 241–259.

Cullen, A., & Hodgetts, D. (2001). Unemployment as illness: An exploration of accounts voiced by the unemployed in Aotearoa/New Zealand. *Analyses of Social Issues and Public Policy, 1*(1), 33–51.

Dambrun, M., & Dubuy, A. L. (2014). A positive psychology intervention among long-term unemployed people and its effects on psychological distress and well-being. *Journal of Employment Counseling, 51*(2), 75–88.

Dassinger, J. (2013). Managing the unemployed no more: Renewing Union adjustment through pedagogy of resistance. *The Review of Education, Pedagogy and Cultural Studies, 35*(3), 217–229. 10.1080/10714413.2013.799365

Dean, M. (1995). Governing the unemployed self in an active society. *Economy and Society, 24*(4), 559–583. 10.1080/03085149500000025

Dean, M. (2010). *Governmentality: Power and rule in modern society* (2nd edition). SAGE.

Deleuze, G. (1992). What is a dispositif? In T. Armstrong (Ed.), *Michel Foucault, Philosopher: Essays*. Harvester Wheatsheaf.

Dreyfus, H., & Rabinow, P. (1983). *Michel Foucault: Beyond structuralism and hermeneutics* (2nd edition). The University of Chicago Press.

Esher House. (n.d.). Esher House: Key information. Retrieved 22 October 2021 from http://esherhouse.org/about-us/#key-information.

Flynn, T. (2005). Foucault's mapping of history. In G. Gutting (Ed.), *The Cambridge Companion to Foucault.*Cambridge University Press.

Forrester, J. (1992). Critical ethnography: On fieldwork in a Habermasian way. In M. Alvesson and H. Willmott (Eds.), *Critical Management Studies* (pp. 46–65). Sage.

Forsey, M. G. (2010). Ethnography as participant listening. *Ethnography, 11*(4), 58–572. 10.1177/1466138110372587

Foucault, M. (1980). Confessions of the flesh. In C. Gordon (Ed.), *Power/knowledge: Selected Interviews and Other Writings, 1972–1977*. Pantheon Books.

Foucault, M. (1985). *The history of sexuality, vol. 2: The use of pleasure* (trans. by Robert Hurley). Pantheon Books.

Foucault, M. (1991a). Politics and the study of discourse. In G. Burchell, C. Gordon, & P. Miller (Eds.), *The Foucault Effect: Studies in Governmentality with Two Lectures and an Interview with Michel Foucault* (pp. 753–772). The University of Chicago Press.

Foucault, M. (1991b). Questions of method. In G. Burchell, C. Gordon, & P. Miller (Eds.), *The Foucault Effect: Studies in Governmentality with Two Lectures and an Interview with Michel Foucault* (pp. 73–86). The University of Chicago Press.

Foucault, M. (2002). *The archaeology of knowledge* (trans. by Alan Sheridan). Taylor & Francis Ltd. (Originally published in 1972).

Foucault, M. (2003a). What is critique? In P. Rabinow & N. Rose (Eds.), *The Essential Foucault: Selections from Essential Works of Foucault, 1954–1984* (pp. 263–278). The New York Press.

Foucault, M. (2003b). So it is important to think? In P. Rabinow & N. Rose (Eds.), *The Essential Foucault: Selections from Essential Works of Foucault, 1954–1984* (pp. 170–173). The New York Press.

Foucault, M. (2003c). The subject and power. In P. Rabinow & N. Rose (Eds.), *The Essential Foucault: Selections from Essential Works of Foucault, 1954–1984* (pp. 126–144). The New York Press.

Foucault, M. (2003d). Polemics, politics and problematisations. In P. Rabinow & N. Rose (Eds.), *The Essential Foucault: Selections from Essential Works of Foucault, 1954–1984* (pp. 18–24). The New York Press.

Foucault, M. (2003e). The ethics of the concern of the self as a practice of freedom. In P. Rabinow & N. Rose (Eds.), *The Essential Foucault: Selections from Essential Works of Foucault, 1954–1984* (pp. 25–41). The New York Press.

Foucault, M. (2008). *The birth of biopolitics: Lectures at the Collège de France, 1978–1979.* (trans. Graham Burchell). Palgrave Macmillan.

Friedli, L., & Stern, R. (2015). Positive affect as coercive strategy: Conditionality, activation and the role of psychology in UK government welfare programmes. *Medical Humanities, 41*, 40–47.

Fryer, D., Marley, C., & Stambe, R. (2020). The reproduction of compliant labour power through (re)constitution of the child and adult subject: Critical knowledge-work. *Awry: Journal of Critical Psychology, 1*(1), 35–49.

Fryer, D., & Stambe, R. (2014). Neo-liberal austerity and unemployment: Critical psychological issues. *The Psychologist, 27*(4), 244–248.

Henriques, J., Hollway, W., Urwin, C., Couze, V., & Walkerdine, V. (1984). *Changing the subject: Psychology, social regulation and subjectivity.* Methuen.

Hook, D. (2010). *Foucault, Psychology and the analytics of power.* Palgrave MacMillan.

Jackson, A. Y., & Mazzei, L. A. (2012). *Thinking with theory in qualitative research: Viewing data across multiple perspectives.* Routledge.

Jones, A. (1997). Teaching poststructuralist feminist theory in education: Student resistances. *Gender & Education, 9*(3), 261–269. 10.1080/09540259721240

Kendall, G. (2011). Foucauldian approaches to the self. In A. Elliott (Ed.), *Routledge Handbook of Identity Studies.* Routledge.

Koopman, M. Y., Pieterse, M. E., Bohlmeijer, E. T., & Drossaert, C. H. (2017). Mental health promoting interventions for the unemployed: A systematic review of applied techniques and effectiveness. *International Journal of Mental Health Promotion, 19*(4), 202–223.

Law, J. (2004). *After method: Mess in social science research.* Routledge.

Li, T. (2003). Situating resource struggles: Concepts for empirical analysis. *Economic and Political Weekly, 38*(48) 5120–5128. doi:10.111/joac.12109.
Liu, S., Huang, J. L., & Wang, M. (2014). Effectiveness of job search interventions: A meta-analytic review. *Psychological Bulletin, 140*(4), 1009–1041.
McAvoy, J. (2015). From ideology to feeling: Discourse, emotion and an analytic synthesis. *Qualitative Research in Psychology, 12*(1), 22–33.
McDonald, C., & Marston, G. (2005). Workfare as welfare: Governing unemployment in the advanced liberal state. *Critical Social Policy, 25*(3), 374–401. 10.1177/0261018305054077
McNamee, S. (2015). Radical presence: Alternatives to the therapeutic state. *European Journal of Psychotherapy & Counselling, 17*(4), 373–383. 10.1080/13642537.2015.1094504
Mol, A. (1999). Ontological politics: A word and some questions. In J. Law & J. Hassard (Eds.), *Actor Network Theory and After*. Blackwell.
Mol, A. (2008). *The logic of care: Health and the problem of patient choice*. Routledge.
Nic Giolla Easpaig, B., Fryer, D., Linn, S., & Humphrey, R. (2014). A queer-theoretical approach to community health psychology. *Journal of Health Psychology, 19*, 117–125. doi:10.1177/1359105313500259
Parker, I. (2005). *Qualitative psychology: Introducing radical research*. Open University Press.
Penz, O., Sauer, B., Gaitcsh, M., Hofbauer, J., & Glinser, B. (2017). Post-bureaucratic encounters: Affective labour in public employment services. *Critical Social Policy, 37*(4), 540–560. 10.1177/0261018316681286
Rabinow, P., & Rose, N. (2003). Introduction: Foucault today. In P. Rabinow & N. Rose (Eds.), *The Essential Foucault: Selections from Essential Works of Foucault, 1954–1984* (pp. vii–xxxv). The New York Press.
Reddy, W. M. (2001). *The navigation of feeling: A framework for the history of emotions*. Cambridge University Press.
Rimke, H. (2016). Introduction – mental and emotional distress as a social justice issue: Beyond psychocentrism. *Studies in Social Justice, 10*(1), 4–7.
Rose, N. (1996). *Inventing ourselves: Psychology, power and personhood*. Cambridge University Press.
Rose, N. (1999a). *Governing the soul: The shaping of the private self* (2nd edition). Taylor & Frances/Routledge.
Rose, N. (1999b). *Powers of freedom: Reframing political thought*. Cambridge University Press.
Rose, N., O'Malley, P., & Valverde, M. (2006). Governmentality. *Annual Review of Law Social Sciences, 2*, 83–104. 10.1146/annurev.lawsocsci.2.081805.105900
St Pierre, E. A. (2011a). Refusing human being in humanist qualitative inquiry. In N. K. Denzin & M. D. Giardina (Eds.), *Qualitative Inquiry and Global Crises*. Left Coast Printing Inc.
St Pierre, E. A. (2011b). Post qualitative research: The critique and the coming after. In N. K. Denzin & Y. S. Lincoln (Eds.), *The Sage Handbook of Qualitative Research* (pp. 611–627). Sage Publications.
Stambe, R. (2020). Becoming 'unemployed': Mapping and (re)constituting subjectivity within jobactive. PhD Thesis, Institute for Social Science Research, The University of Queensland. 10.14264/uql.2020.97
Stambe, R., & Fryer, D. (2014). Photovoice: Doing assessed research as an undergraduate from a critical standpoint. *SAGE Research Method Cases,* retrieved from http://dx.doi.org/10.4135/978144627305013509770
Teghtsoonian, K. (2016). Methods, discourse, activism: Comparing institutional ethnography and governmentality. *Critical Policy Studies, 10*(3), 330–347.

Teo. T. (2009). Philosophical concerns in critical psychology. In D. Fox, I. Prilleltensky, & S. Austin (Eds.), *Critical Psychology: An Introduction* (2nd edition) (pp. 36–54). SAGE Publications Ltd.

Valverde, M. (2004). Experience and truth-telling in a post-humanist world: A Foucauldian contribution to feminist reflection. In D. Taylor & K. Vintges (Eds.), *Feminism and the Final Foucault*. University of Illinois Press.

van Berkel, R. (2013). Triple activation: Introducing welfare-to-work into Dutch Social Assistance. In E. Z. Brodkin & G. Marston (Eds.), *Work and the Welfare State: Street-level Organizations and Workfare Politics*. Georgetown University Press.

Walker, C., Hanna, P., Cunningham, L., & Ambrose, P. (2014). A kind of mental warfare: An economy of affect in the UK debt collection industry. *The Australian Community Psychologist, 26*(2), 54–67.

Wetherell, M. (2012). *Affect and Emotion: A New Social Science Understanding*. Sage.

Young, M. I. (1988). Five faces of oppression. *The Philosophical Forum, 19*(4), 270–290.

3

A CRITIQUE OF METHODS

The problem of (researching) unemployment

In the last chapter, I outlined a research strategy based on tracing the apparatus that produces unemployment. In this chapter, I want to read the literature on unemployment differently, including the research methods that produce this knowledge. It is a pertinent question in today's context where 'quarantine unemployment' has resulted in periods of high unemployment and simultaneously created spaces for dominant narratives about how best to 'resolve' the detrimental impact of worklessness. To go beyond these discussions, we also need to review the literature from a different starting point.

Arguably, a literature review requires a form of analysis or interpretation of the body of research done from a specific frame of reference. Literature reviews often require researchers to assess the literature within 'in-house assumptions' to assess the quality of research and to suggest future research. However, we can also take a step back and assess literature following 'field assumptions' or, in more Foucauldian terms, the discourse that establishes what can be said and taken seriously (Alvesson & Sandberg, 2013, pp. 53–56). In this chapter, I suggest this can be achieved by thinking through 'problematisations'.

Problematisation as a 'way of thinking' and a method, shows how an object becomes a problem and thus an object of thought. The task for the researcher is to uncover *how* unemployment is constituted as a problem. Studies exploring such problematisations focus on the "games of truth" (Foucault 1985, p. 6) that, through historical processes, constitute our experiences. The analytical focus is on how it is possible to think about and manage people. This includes the technologies invented to identify and solve these problems, the expert professional subjects created and endorsed to enforce and legitimise particular truths, and the ideal subjectivities that are the telos of governing (Foucault, 2003a). Using this

DOI: 10.4324/9781003112518-3

framework will prevent endorsing any literature as 'truth'; ensuring the focus is on understanding the processes related to the production of truth.

The examination of method also needs to extend to research that is usually positioned as 'critical'. I discuss literature on 'how to research' unemployment from two standpoints: psychology and governmentality research. I begin with psychological research on unemployment and discuss the concern with causality. I explain why I positioned my research as deliberately moving away from such fixations and present governmentality as an alternative. However, there have been sustained debates in governmentality studies about archival research and social science fieldwork methods and I also outline some of these arguments. By examining issues of method I highlight the productivity of research methods in terms of both producing a certain kind of unemployment and reifying objects under investigation.

How it 'feels' to be unemployed

In the psychological literature, the concern about 'unemployment' extends beyond economic issues. As Dooley (2003) opined, the economy is "one of the most important social environments that affect[s] wellbeing" (p. 9). Indeed, for decades psychological research has investigated the negative 'consequences' of 'unemployment' for 'psychological health' (for example see Fryer & Payne, 1986; Paul & Moser, 2009; Wanberg, 2012). 'Psychological health' is generally understood by these researchers as "an individual's emotional and mental wellbeing, ability to function in society, and capacity to meet the demands of day-to-day life" (Wanberg, 2012, p. 371). Studies claim that unemployment is associated with individual misery and mental health problems including anxiety, depression, negative self-esteem, dissatisfaction with life, social dislocation, community dysfunction and population morbidity (Fryer, 2019).

This body of literature also contends that the impact of 'unemployment' includes poor physical wellbeing (McKee-Ryan et al., 2005); worsens health inequalities (Acevedo et al., 2020); experiences of stigma (Karren & Sherman, 2012), which are exacerbated when receiving an unemployment allowance (Keily & Butterworth, 2013); and increased suicidality (Classen & Dunn, 2012). The body of literature leans towards asserting that unemployment *causes* despair. The most recent and widely cited statistically sophisticated meta-review from Paul and Moser (2009) analysed 237 cross-sectional and 87 longitudinal studies across several disciplines and English and German language articles. The authors reported that the longitudinal results "endorse the hypothesis that unemployment not only correlates with, but also causes mental health impairments" (p. 276).

The claim emerging from recent literature reviews that unemployment 'causes' distress is mostly uncontroversial (see Fryer, 2019; Wood & Burchell, 2018). What is contested in the literature is 'how' and 'why' unemployment is associated with misery for many people. Unpacking how and why unemployment is so stressful connects to how psychologists intend to remedy this distress. I argue that it is essential to interrogate the fundamental research on the psychology of unemployment and the individual intervention strategies to rethink unemployment.

For example, McKee-Ryan et al. (2005) situate the reason for unemployment distress in poor individual coping strategies, so teaching better coping strategies is the solution. For others, the problem of unemployment misery is partly explained through lack of resilience, and thus they claim intervention should focus on activating the individual to 'bounce back' (Paul & Moser, 2009). Both of these approaches place responsibility on the individual to adjust. The focus also obscures other important factors related to the constitution of 'unemployment' and how 'unemployment' can be experienced. These psychologised discourses that blame the individual rely on the idea of the 'modernist individual' or that a person is a stable, consistent, rational and separate entity from the structures and environment. Examining psychological literature on 'unemployment' and the discourses used is important here since it provides an avenue for unpacking how 'unemployment' has come to have meaning and can illuminate how these discourses function.

Unemployment has not always been within the scope of psychologists. Walters (2000) argued that unemployment was an issue of economics and policy in the United Kingdom until the 1930s. At this time, the experiences of unemployment became visible because researchers started looking at lived experiences rather than relying purely on statistical explorations. Walters claims the focus started to shift away from structural explanations and the unemployed themselves became observable, knowable and eventually, governable through the administration of unemployment via the welfare state.

One of the fundamental studies in this period was the Marienthal study (Jahoda et al., 1971). The study captured the mundane daily activities of villagers who had lost work. The Marienthal study was situated in the Austrian village of 'Marienthal' during the Great Depression (Jahoda et al., 1971). The village's main employer, a local factory, closed down and subsequently, 70% of the village (bar some, for example, the local butcher) were unemployed. I will discuss the study's research design in the next section, but it is important to note that the researchers positioned their work as being about the unemployed community and not the unemployed individual. The study's key insight was that "unemployment leads to a state of apathy" (Lazarsfeld, 1971, vii) whereby the unemployed did not participate in the limited amount of opportunities available to them. Other terms used by the authors to describe the unemployed include "under the dole system he [sic] is destitute and idle" (p. x, emphasis in original), "feeling of irrevocability and hopelessness" (p. 79) or "misery" (p. 46) and they discussed 'motivation' and 'attitudes'. They did not, however, use words we would expect in today's psychological research on unemployment such as 'depressed', 'anxious' and 'stressed'. Additionally, as Fryer (2019) noted, early research on unemployment connected misery to the experience of financial instability and impoverishment, not unemployment per se.

The Marienthal study became a highly influential work in the psychology of unemployment research. Fleck (2002) argued that the Marienthal study spearheaded the way for subsequent research that examined and demonstrated the effects of unemployment on individuals and communities. In particular, deprivation theory was developed (partly) from this study (Jahoda, 1982). Jahoda's (1982) deprivation theory posits that employment has both manifest and latent functions. The manifest function is financial remuneration. The latent functions are psychological: time structure, activity, status and identity, collective purpose and social contact. The deprivation theory thus establishes the problems of unemployment to be integral to the inner workings of the unemployed while simultaneously downplaying the external factors, such as poverty. The deprivation theory remains the most influential theory on unemployment (Sage, 2019; Wood & Burchell, 2018).

Deprivation theory and its influence on work and worklessness should be situated within a Westernised lens of the world of work. Even though the deprivation theory has been central to theories about the importance and meaningfulness of work and the suffering experienced by those without work across time and place, there have been some caveats. Research findings on unemployment and the findings are often generalised from one context, mostly in the Global North, to the rest of the world (Wood & Burchell, 2018). Although there is evidence that unemployment is a negative experience in non-Western countries like such as China (Yang, 2015) and South Africa (du Toit et al., 2018) generalising from Western countries is problematic. Notably, in labour markets that do not reflect a Westernised labour market that revolves around the standard employment relation and welfare provisions. For example, in Nambia, researchers have not found deprivation theory to be a useful explanatory framework because of the different labour market conditions (see Gonzo & Plattner, 2003). Many people, especially in societies that rely on 'family work' connected to domestic, agricultural or informal work, will not 'count' as employed, and are deemed as 'unemployed' per the categorizations used in Western research and policy (Burchell et al., 2016). Many of the psychological notions used to make sense of unemployment are also deeply embedded within a Western framework and should be interrogated as such.

Research on unemployment from the 1980s became increasingly psychological partly due to a resurgence of interest in the topic following from the recessions in the 1970s and 1980s. This renewed interest was also partly politically motivated to challenge the public and political claims that the unemployed were 'skivvers' (see Fryer, 2019). The research on unemployment that was produced in this period continued the framing of work and worklessness as psychological, within the Western discourse. Unemployment was turned into scores about 'wellbeing' from the General Health Questionnaire (which was a favourite in this field of research, see Fryer, 1992), and other scales such as the Beck Depression Inventory (Feather & Barber, 1983) or the State Anxiety Questionnaire (Lev-Wiesel & Kaufman, 2004). This literature does not often acknowledge that the psychometric tools used to 'measure' the 'feelings' and 'experiences' of the unemployed are hardly objective or universal. There is limited discussion about how these tools are embedded within social norms about the role of work, the subject, and rarely mention the historical context (Cromby & Willis, 2014).

Although scholars have noted the predominance of studying symptoms rather than clinical diagnosis in the literature (Catalano et al., 2011), the problem of the 'affects' of unemployment is rendered psychological through the knowledges and devices used to study these effects. As Rose (1999) points out, assessments render individual differences visible and technical. By presenting the human experience as calculable and objective, these assessments are positioned as close to the 'truth' of the experience and thus are formed in, and reinforce, the authority of psychological knowledge. Some scholars go as far as to argue that "psychiatric diagnosis is a professional reification about human misery, not a fact" (Pilgrim & Bentall, 1999, p. 271). Importantly, what these assessments operationalise (and go on to 'measure') can be understood as certain 'truths' that are socially, culturally and historically contingent and material. These assessments form part of a broader apparatus, so what can be articulated as 'experience' is constructed by and through discourse, institutions and practices, of which experience is the effect.

As well as producing a particular kind of experience by situating unemployment within a 'regime of truth' (psychology), there are other assumptions about the organisation of the social world that underpin this body of research that needs to be unpacked. Jahoda (1982) (whose work was influenced by Austro-marxism and psychoanalysis) admitted that employment is the only institution able to provide all of the functions required for subjective wellbeing in the labour market. She envisioned a time when employment could be replaced by something else, but that would not be for "about 500 years" (Jahoda & Ernst as cited in Wacker, 2012, p. 129). Her work and the Marienthal study emphasise the productive self, reproducing a moral discourse by valorising the importance of work in a person's life (Cole, 2007). Work is assumed to be 'normal', diminishing any non-work experiences despite research that suggests non-job-related activities have beneficial or 'anti-depressive' effects (Haworth, 1997). Parenthood and caring work is often presented as an example of such beneficial non-work (Nordenmark & Strandh, 1999). For Cole, the Marienthal research depicted the unemployed as 'doing nothing' (as opposed to doing 'non-work' such as caring or engaging in political activity), which he argued misread people's attempts to survive unemployment. The social imaginary that the unemployed are demoralised and passive underpins common sense notions about the problem of unemployment, but also is evident in scholarly attempts to define and understand unemployment.

Scholars have also further critiqued Jahoda's emphasis on the psychological aspects of unemployment (Cole, 2007). Fryer (1992), for example, counteracted the over-reliance on latent functions in Jahoda's work by shifting focus back onto financial and material deprivation and the implications for agency. However, both Fryer and Jahoda still place more focus on the importance of work in a person's life and place little emphasis on individual differences (Ezzy, 1993). So too do other theories on the effects of unemployment. For example, Paul and Moser's (2009) incongruence theory relies on the assumption that people are committed to and want to work. This assumption is required for the authors to assert that the incongruence between work commitment and actual reality impacts the person in psychologised ways. While Paul and Moser (2009) accounted for the influence of the Protestant work ethic, they do not critically evaluate the assumptions underpinning the meaning of work and what this means for how we think about current or possible working relations.

I argue that such commonsensical notions about the meaning of work are also important to unpack when examining psychological research that characteristics distress of unemployment as psychologised notions of 'depression' and such forth. The solutions to unemployment rectify the inner mind of the unemployed, (through psychological interventions such as cognitive behavioural therapy (CBT), Henderson & Muller, 2013, or programs that supposedly improve 'positive affect' and thus job-seeking behaviours, Turban et al., 2013). Additionally, the coping solutions presented emphasise re-employment and the 'naturalness' of employment by encouraging people to cope with unemployment (Shuring et al., 2017). Placing the focus on 'coping' as a common solution, never challenges the institution of employment and leaves untroubled some of the problems of being employed, simplistically labelling any work as 'good' (Ezzy, 1993; Kalleberg, 2011). It also misses the complexities of precarious employment that are prioritised in a 'flexible' economy (Standing, 2014) and extends theoretical assertions made based on the standard employment relations (such as deprivation theory) which may not be appropriate in economics that include the gig economy and zero-hour contracts (Wood & Burchell, 2018). As well as essentialising and moralising paid work (as opposed to other forms of work), research tends to overestimate the influence of individual-led coping strategies without contextualising the role of social norms or policy implications for individuals or communities (Roex & Rözer, 2018). Unemployment becomes a (psychological) problem of the individual/leaving unexamined how un/employment is produced.

In this way, psychologised and individualised knowledges about unemployment, how it 'feels', and how it can be remedied (through employment) is part of the knowledge base of the *jobactive* apparatus. These psy knowledges 'about' unemployment assists with, the dominant discourses of 'activation' and 'work first' (or welfare-through-work). For a post-disciplinary perspective on researching unemployment, these psychologised knowledges and/or research practices to understand the 'experience' of unemployment need closer examination in terms of how it problematises 'unemployment', rendering it an object of thought.

Causation vs individual drift: The problem of method

What is possible to 'know' about unemployment is related to how it is possible to 'know'. The Marienthal study stands out amongst psychological research since it employed a sociological method and the study is methodologically impressive. One of the principal investigators of the Marienthal study, Lazarsfeld (1971, p. xi), explained that it was his dissatisfaction with the unemployment figures at the time and how unemployed life was being described, in causal terms, in popular media partly inspired the research.

The study used a mixed-methods type design, which they called 'immersion'. Immersion refers to an in-depth and highly detailed collection of information regarding various aspects of the Marienthal community. Lazarsfeld argued this was achieved through case studies, times sheets, meal records, questionnaires, "solicited reports" of the lived experience of the unemployed and "unobtrusive measures" of observation (Lazarsfeld, 1971, p. xiv). The researchers wanted an eclectic approach since "[m]ore description was not enough. To 'get behind' it, a variety of data had to be collected on any issue under investigation, just as the true position of a distant object can be found only through triangulation, by looking at it from different sides and direction" (p. xiv). Despite the 'objective' approach to the study, they nevertheless highlighted the specificity of the research and did not make broad generalisations. The study also engaged in 'action' elements such as running activities for the townspeople.

Fryer and Payne (1986) identified three other significant studies in the 1930s that were occupied with the subject of 'unemployment'; those of Bakke, Subsistence Production Society (as described in Jahoda, 1982) and the Pilgrim Trust. Although varying in method, each study described the negative consequences of 'unemployment' sullenness, despondency, demoralisation (Bakke, as cited in Fryer & Payne, pp. 242–243); loss of identity; anxiety, depression, apathy, isolation and loneliness. Fryer and Payne stated that both the Bakke and the Subsistence Production Society studies emphasised the pre-unemployment conditions. For Bakke, this was the "qualities of the working man ... as a result of the social heritage of the individual", and for Jahoda it was the thought habits that were "steeped in the traditions of capitalism" (as cited in Fryer & Payne, p. 244). These approaches contrast starkly with the approach favoured by psychologists today.

In these three studies, there is a connection between the broader societal and ideological processes and their impact on individual formation and the acceptable ways an unemployed person can react to worklessness. However, according to Walters (2000), the Pilgrim Trust study was interested in the personal aspects which could explain long-term unemployment, as "long unemployment is one of those problems where cause and effect are inextricably mixed ... for instance, long unemployment may itself make a man unemployable" (Pilgrim Trust, as cited in Walters, 2000, p. 86). Walters argued that the Pilgrim Trust suggested that a potential cause of unemployment, the 'problem', was the effect of unemployment: demoralisation.

Psychological research has been concerned with determining causality. The 'gold standard' research method for unemployment is the prospective longitudinal study (Dooley & Prause, 2004). This particular research method is presented as the gold standard because of a nagging issue within the literature known as the 'social causation vs individual drift' problem (Jefferies et al., 2011). The problem is thus the concern with causality, framing the issue in methodological terms. Wanberg (2012) noted that "a great focus of recent on unemployment and wellbeing has been on issues of causality" (p. 371) and indeed studies tend to be preoccupied with the need to separate the 'egg from the chicken', which is indeterminable from cross-sectional designs (Ronchetti & Terriau, 2019). The key question that underlies many studies is this: is unemployment caused by poor subjective wellbeing (depressed affect, stress, anxiety, low self-esteem) or is poor subjective wellbeing caused by unemployment (again depressed affect, stress, low self-esteem)?

Connected to this problematisation of cause is the problem of moderating factors. As the argument goes, unemployment is detrimental to people in a general sense, it is still experienced differently by people. Thus, the problem of 'what caused what' is further complicated by age, the welfare state, gender, marital status, duration of unemployment and so on (for meta-analysis see Paul & Moser, 2009). McKee (2009) noted in their analysis of the literature there are around 100 different variables correlating with different indicators of psychological and physical wellbeing during unemployment. It should be noted that these 'categories' do not describe the world, but are charged with power-knowledge relations and are contested. The literature is not always clear on the differences between sex and gender, for example. Women are often positioned as being less severely impacted by unemployment compared to men without a sophisticated understanding of the gender regime, labour markets, and what this then means for how we think about unemployment (see Strandh et al., 2012). Also, moderating factors are more than a way of categorising people. The processes of categorisation also help to describe the problem in specific ways, and are infused with social norms or naturalised ways of understanding the social world. However, these are not the main issues of methodological concern when discussing causality.

The issue of causality is a complicated issue for research design. Cross-sectional studies (which dominate the literature) tend to assume, by comparison of means, a point of 'normality', in the literature this is a healthy employed sample. This in itself is a point of contention in terms of whether people have meaningful, steady, good jobs (Fryer, 1997; Ronchetti & Terriau, 2019). Furthermore, being unemployed can lead to poor mental health (social causation), but the 'scarring' effects mean a person may struggle to find or keep employment (individual drift) (Fryer, 1992), which compounds effects and makes determining the direction of any casualty difficult. There is also the possibility of some other event leading to decreased emotional wellbeing which precedes becoming unemployed (Diette et al., 2012). The literature is filled with these issues and debates underpinned by reductionist frameworks and the pursuit of causal relationships.

Of course, any questions that we ask about a topic in the form of a research question come with embedded conceptual baggage, including the issue of what questions can be asked when conducting research. The problem of causality is only conceivable as a problem within a framework that considers 'unemployment' and 'psychological wellbeing' as objects accessible and quantifiable through certain systematic methods. Traditional psychological research is "committed to natural-scientific, experimental-statistical or empirical-statistical methodology" (Teo, 2009).

The argument goes that these methods, when administered adequately through deductive reasoning (hypothetical deductive model), and controlling for mediating variables, have a potential for causal claims to be made. These methods are constructed within modernist, scientific discourses which assume that via careful analysis, observation and measurement, the human condition and experience can be reduced to fundamental principles which can universally explain phenomena. The focus is on ensuring the method is 'right' for the 'truth' or 'facts' to be uncovered.

The point here is not to make the mistake of oversimplifying very sophisticated statistical and design methods. My primary interest is not whether these approaches are 'wrong' (for they are another way of producing 'truth') but how they are accorded the status of truth and how these truths function. To unpack these issues, I argue psychological research can be usefully examined using questions that are often excluded from the research design, such as, who benefits from this knowledge? How is this knowledge dovetailed into specific economic, political, social and historical matrixes? What kinds of assumptions constitute the possibility of doing this type of research, and that is also reproduced by the research?

We can use such questions about the assumptions, impact and politics of research to further unpack psychological research on unemployment. Much of psychological research is built upon the assumptions that the inner workings of the mind can be mapped scientifically, although Skinner's behaviourism is an exception (Parker, 2007). Nevertheless, for unemployment research to use psychological assessments, many of which require self-reporting, there is an assumption that an individual can access their own thoughts and accurately transpose these into the pre-given template of questions and Likert scales. Such methods further assume that the subject is a humanist subject, as previously noted, one that is rational, static and unitary. Potentially reducing the complexity which we 'are' or the fluidity of our selves/worlds and potential for being otherwise. The unemployed could be 'acknowledged' as expressing certain distress, and their subjectivity becomes 'stuck' as the distressed unemployed.

Psychological research reinforces the idea that unemployment is a problem of the individual. This is so even if we ignore some of the problematic assumptions of psychological research and agree that, with some caveats, the bulk of research has since the 1930s suggested that unemployment 'causes' mental distress (Fryer, 2012). The theories presented to explain distress and the solutions presented enforce an individualistic understanding of unemployment and tend to underplay how employment is a powerful social norm, which means those that cannot claim this identity feel judged and stigmatised (Sage, 2019). While researchers have noted that some employment arrangements such as underemployment, or not receiving enough work hours, insecure work and the gig economy have equal, sometimes worse, negative consequences for people (Davis & Hoyt, 2020); Paul and Moser (2009) claimed the solution to the harmful impact of 'unemployment' should involve intervention to hasten re-employment. Paul and Moser stated the way to do this is through isolating the characteristics of the 'resilient' and motivated unemployed in order to provide training of such 'characteristics' or 'skills' for the unemployed who are deemed to be not 'coping' as effectively, in terms of both managing the experiences of 'unemployment' and engaging in job-seeking behaviours. Psychology here is implicated in producing social relationships, and institutional issues are reduced to the properties of individuals, potentially blaming the victim. The unemployed are divided from the employed and through positioning employment as the best solution to unemployment, conversations about the problems of the labour market and work are sidelined. Not least how useful it is for the labour market to have surplus labour that is continually working upon itself to 'cope' and prepare to (re)enter the workforce.

In rethinking the problem of unemployment, I want to move past positioning unemployment as a lack of employment and instead study how the experience of unemployment is possible or how it is "an actively produced category" (Boland & Griffin, 2015, p. 2). As discussed at the beginning of this book, the welfare state and ES in Australia are integral to this unemployment production. I position the spaces of ES to be a crucible where various heterogeneous elements, such as administrative practices, policy, questionnaires and training programs are laid out together to change the way the unemployed act. ES also opens up spaces for different/new professionals to establish their expertise (for example, 'welfare applied for positive psychology programs' see esherhouse.org) or provide new market opportunities. Governmentality is a useful framework for studying ES, but as I discuss below, while it does circumvent some of the issues in psychological research there are still methodological debates that require examination.

The problem with governmentality studies

In this section, I will explore some of the commentary highlighting the shortcomings of governmentality research. I will pay particular attention to the suggestion that governmentality research is dominated by archival research that misses the nuances, misadventures and contradictions that can be located 'on the ground'. The concern about overreliance on secondary data also connects to arguments about incorporating a realist ontology into governmentality studies. The argument against archival research and for fieldwork, including from a realist position, highlights how critical psychology research on unemployment needs to move into a post-disciplinary space to engage seriously with debates in other disciplinary spaces to carve out research that is theoretically coherent with the broader aims of a project.

Limitations of governmentality studies

Governmentality studies bring together a multiplicity of different scholars, attached to different disciplines and herein there are several lines of methodological debate. I will discuss a key criticism of governmentality studies that are relevant to my own design: the problem of just using the archive or secondary data. Researchers present several main concerns from the assumed overreliance on secondary data: oversimplification of subjectification, production of cookie-cutter explanations and grand narratives.

In terms of subjectivity, the argument goes that overreliance on secondary data leads to a 'prose' where subjectification is assumed to be a direct effect of discourse (such as policy), sidelining the potential for agency and losing the ambiguity of subjectification (Barnett et al., 2008; Binkley, 2011; Clarke, 2006). Further, Walkerdine and Bansel (2010) noted a proclivity in this literature to 'read off' discourse. These authors suggest this 'reading' creates difficulties because our subjectivity is constituted as one aspect of a web or matrix of relations, continually shifting, developed in historically and temporally located spaces. Hence, they argued that researchers need to consider the location and temporality of practices when discussing discursive effects. Their research interviewed redundant/unemployed persons in South Wales, United Kingdom and Sydney, Australia. Their findings demonstrated that Sydneysiders had a more individualistic explanation of their unemployment than the South Welshmen, which the authors suggest was contingent on the place-based manifestations of neoliberal discourse.

Rose et al. (2006, p. 97) stated that while governmentality helps identify rationalities, problematisations and technologies, it also lends itself to a 'cookie-cutter' explanation style. This is where explanatory devices subsume entire programs without clarifying between elements that may conflict. Li (2007) posited that governmentality literature misses the misadventures, conflicts and tensions in policy implementation. Particularly about the work done to smooth over this tension. Subsequently, researchers need to pay attention to the politics, practices, attempts to resolve conflict, contradictions, and how governmentality rationalities co-exist with the logic of sovereignty.

Other researchers have discussed similar concerns, such as difficulties in the assumption that one type of power is displaced by another (e.g. from sovereign to disciplinary) power configurations that are shifting and messy (Collier, 2009). Brady (2014) argued that this tendency is noted in governmentality literature, particularly about treating neoliberalism as a grand narrative. As a consequence, "when rationalities and technologies are characterised as singular, clear and settled in ways they are not" (p. 24) then power relations appear to be exhaustive and complete. This is counter to the project of governmentality, which itself is tied to processes of critique (Foucault, 2003b). Walters (2012) also encouraged researchers to merge governmentality with methods such as ethnography to attune to the "unwritten and unsaid ways in which things work by not working" (p. 146).

Researching 'ethnographically'

Since my research used a form of ethnography, I will focus on discussions that champion this approach as methodology. Ethnographers merge 'top-down' and 'bottom-up' research practices to preclude coherences in political rationalities, power relations or apparatuses (see Biehl & McKay, 2012; Clarke, 2017). Bringing these together means governmentality research is no longer "abstracted from subjects and spaces" since the bottom-up elements provide an opportunity to study the technologies and rationalities of governing but also the "the evasions, resistances, enablements, exclusions, and/or motivations or individual behaviour which occur alongside and about new forms of contemporary 'government'" (Mitchell, 2006, p. 390). Brady (2014) made a strong case for merging governmentality and ethnography asserting that by ethnographies "beginning with the everyday" they can avoid the "deterministic, homogenous, and static accounts of social transformation" (p. 11).

The risk here however is elements of realism, understood in the broadest sense, can creep back into the research. This includes reintroducing the pre-discursive subjects and reifying objects. Such problems were raised by Dean (2015) who countered Brady's argument by refuting her on several points. Dean stated that he had no objections to scholars diverging from Foucault's work or using ethnography to study 'practice', but he disagreed with Brady's fundamental argument for ethnography. He objected to Brady's claim that ethnography as a method is justified with Foucault's work and the related second claim Brady makes about ethnography having exclusive access to the 'actual practices' of governing. By maintaining an 'epistemological imperialism' for ethnography to address the 'Achilles heel' of governmentality studies, Dean suggested Brady returns to something of 'the real'. Here Dean argued Brady's argument for using ethnography to research the actual practices of governing is decidedly removed from Foucault's work since "Foucault is not seeking to access the complexity of everyday life but the conditions under which we form a knowledge of and seek to govern such domains as everyday life" (p. 359). As Rose (1999, p. 20) argued researching governmentality involves, "asking what authorities of various sorts wanted to happen, about problems defined how, in pursuit of what objectives, through what strategies and techniques". Such governing strategies are types of intervention since political rationalities do not represent the world as it is but "itself constitutes the intellectual processes of the reality which political technologies can then tackle" (Lemke, 2001, p. 191).

Despite the delineation between researching, 'the real' and the constitution of 'the real', there have been explicit calls for drawing on realism in governmentality studies. These call for closer attention to the everyday complexity and context of policy implementation and invite researchers to employ fieldwork-based methods, including mixed-methods (see McKee, 2009). Such contextualisation avoids the supposed overgeneralisations of governmentality studies, including assuming language has a constitutive effect (Lippert & Stenson, 2010). However, engaging in realism in this way has potential methodological traps. According to Larner (2008, p. 23), the challenge is getting the balance between social science methods that "rely on self-evident descriptions" with a governmentality approach that unsettles and denaturalises such concepts to then understand how it functions. This approach raises concerns for researchers interested in critical approaches that are trying to suspend unemployment to unpack how it is produced as an active concept, as I mentioned in the previous chapter. The debates around fieldwork and governmentality, although promising also presented issues that created (meta) theoretical incoherence.

Not all researchers agree that fieldwork methods are necessarily realist. Collier (2013) argued that he uses ethnography as part of wider "arc of inquiry" that serves to focus on problems about or to problematise concepts and to guide further inquiry. Here he suggests that doing this sort of fieldwork can assist with the "grouping of sites and a set of problems that I simply could not have stumbled upon otherwise" (Collier, 2011, p. 29). Brady (2016) drew from this literature that distances itself from realist assumptions by employing an 'ethnographic imagination' that is not a method or a methodology but a 'sensitivity'. While on the surface this approach seemed to overcome issues relating to reifying self-evident descriptions or naive realism, the enactment of research presented other problems around the pre-discursive self. For example, Brady (2011) sophistically develops a governmental approach with ethnography to study "which issues around gender, paid work and care work *service providers recognized* and which issues *they marginalized*, and whether or not these issues matched or differed from official discourses" (p. 273, my emphasis). The focus here subtly moves from examining discourse, what is said, to the inner process of who is speaking, which creates tension for researchers interested in challenging the psy-complex. As I have discussed and will raise again in the sixth chapter, critical research requires the same interrogation that we give psychological research in terms of how knowledge is produced and how it functions.

Concluding comments

This chapter suggested that reviewing psychological and governmental literature requires a critical attitude lest we also leave 'self evident' concepts that we are trying to critique or reproduce such concepts through our methods. Part of this process is thinking about how people are categorised and how that categorisation forms objects, subjects, places, and how these ways of thinking are the effects of research methods, research tools and instruments rather than simply a way of grouping or 'understanding' people.

Research processes and the problems that are prioritised rely on assumptions about the purpose of research and its relation to the production of 'knowledge'. These arguments are not trivial and should be attended to both methodologically but also as a way to unpack research problems and the productivity of research. In the next chapter, I continue to apply this problematisation lens to examine employment services policy, psy and the implications of unemployed subjectivity.

References

Acevedo, P., Mora-Urda, A., & Montero, P. (2020). Social inequalities in health: Duration of unemployment unevenly effects on the health of men and women. *European Journal of Public Health, 30*(2), 305–310.

Alvesson, M., & Sandberg, J. (2013). *Constructing research question: Doing interesting research*. Sage.

Barnett, C., Clarke, N., Cloke, P., & Malpass, A. (2008). The elusive subjects of neo-liberalism: Beyond the analytics of governmentality. *Cultural Studies*, *22*(5), 624–653.

Biehl, J., & McKay, R. (2012). Ethnography as political critique. *Anthropological Quarterly*, *85*(4), 1209–1227.

Binkley, S. (2011). Psychological life as enterprise: Social practice and the government of neo-liberal interiority. *History of the Human Sciences*, *24*(3), 83–102. doi:10.1177/0952695111412877.

Boland, T., & Griffin, R. (2015). Introduction and general remarks. In T. Boland & R. Griffin (Eds.), *The Sociology of Unemployment*. Manchester University Press.

Brady, M. (2011). Researching governmentalities through ethnography: the case of Australian welfare reforms and programs for single parents. *Critical Policy Studies*, *5*, 264–282. 10.1080/19460171.2011.606300

Brady, M. (2014). Ethnographies of neoliberal governmentalities: From the neoliberal apparatus to neoliberalism and governmental assemblages. *Foucault Studies*, *18*, 11–33. 10.22439/fs.v0i18.4649

Brady, M. (2016). Neoliberalism, Governmental Assemblages, And The Ethnographic Imaginary, *Governing Practices: Neoliberalism, governmentality and the ethnographic imaginary* (pp. 3–32). 10.3138/9781487511913-003

Burchell B. J., Coutts A., Hall E., & Pye N. (2016). *Self-employment programmes for young people: A review of the context, policies and evidence*. Employment Working Paper No. 198. International Labour Organisation.

Catalano, R., Goldman-Mellor, S., Saxton, K., Margerison-Zilko, C., Subbaraman, M., LeWinn, K., & Anderson, E. (2011). The health effects of economic decline. *Annual Review of Public Health*, *31*, 431–450. https://pubmed.ncbi.nlm.nih.gov/21054175/

Clarke, A. (2017). Analyzing problematization as a situated practice in critical policy studies: A case study of 'customer focus' policy in urban compliance services. *Critical Policy Studies*, 1–21. 10.1080/19460171.2017.1414619

Clarke, J. (2006). Consumerism and the remaking of state-citizen relations in the UK. In G. Marston & C. McDonald (Eds.), *Analysing Social Policy: A Governmental Approach* (pp. 89–106). Edward Elgar Publishing Ltd.

Classen, T. J., & Dunn, R. A. (2012). The effect of job loss and unemployment duration on suicide risk in the United States: A new look using mass layoffs and unemployment insurance claims. *Health Economic*, *21*(3), 338–350.

Cole, M. (2007). Rethinking unemployment: A challenge to the legacy of Jahoda et al. *Sociology*, *41*(6), 1133–1149.

Collier, S. (2009). Topologies of power: Foucault's analysis of political government beyond 'governmentality'. *Theory, Culture & Society*, *26*(6), 78–108. 10.1177/0263276409347694

Collier, S. J. (2011). *Post-Soviet social: neoliberalism, social modernity, biopolitics*. Princeton University Press.

Collier, S. J. (2013, November). 'Fieldwork as technique for generating what kind of surprise? Thoughts on Post-Soviet Social in light of "Fieldwork/Research"'. Presented at University of California, Irvine, Department of Anthropology. Retrieved from https://stephenjcollier.files.wordpress.com/2014/05/fieldwork-and-surprise.pdf

Cromby, J., & Willis, M. E. H. (2014). Nudging into subjectification: Governmentality and psychometrics. *Critical Social Policy*, *34*(2), 241–259.

Davis, M. E., & Hoyt, E. (2020). A longitudinal study of piece rate and health: Evidence and implications for workers in the US gig economy. *Public Health*, *180*, 1–9.

Dean, M. (2015). Neoliberalism, governmentality, ethnography: A response to Michelle Brady. *Foucault Studies, 20*, 356–366. 10.22439/fs.v0i0.4954
Diette, T. M., Goldsmith, A. R., Hamilton, D., & Darity Jr. W. (2012). Causality in the relationship between mental health and unemployment. In L. D. Appelbaum (Ed.), *Reconnecting to Work: Policies to Mitigate Long-Term Unemployment and Its Consequences*, (pp. 63–94). Upjohn Institute.
Donnell, A. (2015). Unemployment in a time of full employment: Counting and regulating worklessness in mid-twentieth century Australia. *Labour History, 108*, 71–79.
Dooley, D. (2003). Unemployment, underemployment and mental health: Conceptualising employment status as a continuum. *American Journal of Community Psychology, 32*(2), 9–20.
Dooley, D., & Prause, J. (2004). *The social costs of underemployment*. Cambridge University Press.
du Toit, M., Hans De Witte, S., & Van den Broeck, A. (2018). Unemployment experiences in context: A phenomenological study in two townships in South Africa. *Journal of Psychology in Africa, 28*(2), 122–127. 10.1080/14330237.2018.1454575
Ezzy, D. (1993). Unemployment and mental health a critical review. *Social Science and Medicine, 37*(1), 41–52.
Feather, N. T., & Barber, J. G. (1983). Depressive reactions and unemployment. *Journal of Abnormal Psychology, 92*(2), 185–195. doi:10.1037/0021-843X.92.2.185
Fleck, C. (2002). Introduction to the transaction edition. In M. Jahoda, P. F. Lazarsfeld, & H. Zeisel (Eds.), *Marienthal: The Sociography of an Unemployed Community*. Transaction.
Foucault, M. (1985). The use of pleasure: Volume 2 of the history of sexuality. (trans. Robert Hurley). Vintage Books.
Foucault, M. (2003b). Polemics, politics and problematisations. In P. Rabinow & N. Rose (Eds.), *The Essential Foucault: Selections from Essential Works of Foucault, 1954–1984* (pp. 18–24). The New York Press.
Foucault, M. (2003b). What is critique? In P. Rabinow & N. Rose (Eds.), *The Essential Foucault: Selections from Essential Works of Foucault, 1954–1984* (pp. 263–278). The New York Press.
Frings-Sen, M. H. W., Hoving, J. L., Audhoe, S. S., & Sluiter, J. K. (2010). Vocational interventions for unemployed: Effects on work participation and mental distress. A systematic review. *Journal of Occupational Rehabilitation, 20*(1), 1–13. doi:10.1007/s10926-009-9223-y.
Fryer, D., & Payne, R. (1986). Being unemployed: A review of the literature on the psychological experience of unemployment. In C. L. Cooper & I. Robertson (Eds.), *International Review of Industrial and Organisational Psychology*. Wiley.
Fryer, D. (1992). Psychological or material deprivation: Why does unemployment have mental health consequences? In E. Mclaughlin (Ed.), *Understanding Unemployment: New Perspectives on Active Labour Market Policies* (pp. 103–125). SAGE.
Fryer, D. (1997). International perspectives on youth unemployment and mental health: Some central issues. *Journal of Adolescence, 20*(2), 333–342. 10.1006/jado.1997.0089.
Fryer, D. (2012). Critical differences: The development of a community critical psychological perspective on the psychological costs of unemployment. In T. Kieselbach & S. Mannila (Eds.), *Unemployment, Precarious Work and Health: Research and Policy Issues* (pp. 473–489). Springer.
Fryer, D. (2014). Unemployment. In T. Teo (Ed.), *Encyclopaedia of Critical Psychology* (pp. 2031–2036). Springer.
Fryer, D. (2019). Applied social psychology, the neoliberal labour-market subject and critique. In K. Doherty & D. Hodgetts (Eds.), *The SAGE Handbook of Applied Social Psychology*. SAGE.

Ganley, R. (2002). The psychological impact of joblessness. *Australian Social Policy 2002–03*. Australian Government. Retrieved from http://www.forschungsnetzwerk.at/downloadpub/Australia_2002_2003_socialPolicy_2004.pdf#page=183

Gershon, I. (2017). *Down and out in the new economy: How people find (or don't find) work today*. The University of Chicago Press.

Gonzo, W., & Plattner, I. E. (2003). Unemployment in an African country: A psychological perspective. University of Namibia Press.

Goodwin-Smith, I., & Hutchinson, C. (2015). *Beyond supply and demand: Addressing the complexities of workforce exclusion in Australia*. Australian Centre for Community Services.

Haworth, J. T. (1997). *Work, leisure and wellbeing*. Routledge.

Henderson, K. Q., & Muller, J. J. (2013). Addressing mental health and re-employment for unemployed Australian through psychological interventions: An applied study. *Australian Journal of Career Development, 22*(3), 112–120.

Jahoda, M. (1982). *Employment and unemployment: A social-psychological analysis*. Cambridge University Press.

Jahoda, M., Lazarsfeld, P. F., & Zeisel, H. (1971). *Marienthal: The sociography of an unemployed community*. Aldine, Atherton.

Jefferies, B. J. et al. (2011). Associations between unemployment and major depressive disorder: Evidence from an international, prospective study (the predict cohort). *Social Science & Medicine, 73*(11), 1672–1634.

Karren, R., & Sherman, K. (2012). Layoffs and unemployment discrimination: A new stigma. *Journal of Managerial Psychology, 27*(8), 848–863.

Kalleberg, A. L. (2011). *Good Jobs, Bad Jobs: The rise of polarized and precarious employment in the United States 1970s–2000s*. Russell Sage Foundation.

Keily, K. M., & Butterworth, P. (2013). Social disadvantage and individual vulnerability: A longitudinal investigation of welfare receipt and mental health in Australia. *Australian & New Zealand Journal of Psychiatry, 47*(7), 654–666. 10.1177/0004867413484094

Larner, W. (2008). Comments on Stenson's 'Governing the local: Sovereignty, social governance and community safety'. *Social Work and Society – International Online Journal, 6*(1), 21–25. Retrieved from http://www.socwork.net/sws/article/view/87/376.

Lazarsfeld, P. F. (1971) Introduction. In M. Jahoda, P. F. Lazarsfeld, & H. Zeisel (Eds.), *Marienthal: The Sociography of an Unemployed Community*. Aldine, Atherton.

Lemke, T. (2001). 'The birth of bio-politics': Michel Foucault's lecture at the Collège de France on neo-liberal governmentality. *Economy and Society, 30*(2), 190–207.

Lev-Wiesel, R., & Kaufman, R. (2004). Personal characteristics, unemployment, and anxiety among highly educated immigrants. *International Migration, 42*(3), 57–75. doi: 10.111/j.0020-7985.2004.00289.x

Li, T. M. (2007). *The will to improve: Governmentality, development, and the practice of politics*. Duke University Press.

Lippert, R., & Stenson, K. (2010). Advancing governmentality studies: Lessons from social constructionism. *Theoretical Criminology, 14*(4), 473–494. 10.1177/1362480610369328

Liu, S., Huang, J. L., & Wang, M. (2014). Effectiveness of job search interventions: A meta-analytic review. *Psychological Bulletin, 140*(4), 1009–1041. https://pubmed.ncbi.nlm.nih.gov/24588365/

McDonald, C., & Marston, G. (2005). Workfare as welfare: Governing unemployment in the advanced liberal state. *Critical Social Policy, 25*(3), 374–401. 10.1177/0261018305054077

McKee, K. (2009). Post-Foucauldian governmentality: What does it offer critical social policy analysis? *Critical Social Policy, 29*(3), 465–486. 10.1177/0261018309105180

McKee-Ryan, F. M., & Kinicki, A. J. (2002). Coping with job loss: A life-facet perspective. *International Review of Industrial and Organizational Psychology, 17*, 1–30.

Mckee-Ryan, F. M., Song, Z., Wanberg, C. R., & Kinicki, A. J. (2005). Psychological and physical well-being during unemployment: A meta-analytic study. *Journal of Applied Psychology, 90*(1), 53–76.

Mitchell, K. (2006). Neoliberal governmentality in the European Union: Education, training, and technologies of citizenship. *Environment and Planning: Society and Space, 24*(3), 389–407.

Mitchell, W. (2013). Full employment abandoned: The triumph of ideology over evidence. Working paper 02–13 Centre of Full Employment and Equity. Retrieved from http://e1.newcastle.edu.au/coffee/pubs/wp/2013/13-02.pdf

Nordenmark, M., & Strandh, M. (1999). Towards a sociological understanding of mental wellbeing among the unemployed: The role of economic and psychosocial factors. *Sociology, 33*(3), 577–597.

Parker, I. (2007). *Revolution in psychology: Alienation to Emancipation*. Ann Arbour.

Paul, K. I., & Moser, K. (2009). Unemployment impairs mental health: Meta-analyses. *Journal of Vocational Behavior, 74*(3), 264–282. 10.1016/j.jvb.2009.01.001.

Pilgrim, D., & Bentall, R. P. (1999). The medicalisation of misery: A critical realist analysis of the concept of depression. *Journal of Mental Health, 8*(3), 261–274.

Roex, K. L. A., & Rözer, J. J. (2018). The social norm to work and the well-being of the short- and long-term unemployed. *Social Indicators Research, 139*, 1037–1064. 10.1007/s11205-017-1723-0

Ronchetti, J., & Terriau, A. (2019). Impact of unemployment on self-perceived health. *European Journal of Health Economics, 20*, 879–889. 10.1007/s10198-019-01050-5

Rose, N. (1999). *Governing the soul: The shaping of the private* self (2nd edition). Routledge.

Rose, N., O'Malley, P., & Valverde, M. (2006). Governmentality. *Annual Review of Law Social Sciences, 2*, 83–104. 10.1146/annurev.lawsocsci.2.081805.105900

Sage, D. (2019). Unemployment, wellbeing and the power of the work ethic: Implications for social policy. *Critical Social Policy, 39*(2), 205–228.

Shuring, M., Robroek, S. J. W., & Burdorf, A. (2017). The benefits of paid employment among persons with common mental health problems: Evidence for the selection and causation mechanism. *Scandinavian Journal of Work, Environment & Health, 43*(6), 540–549. https://psycnet.apa.org/record/2018-56926-004

Strandh, S., Hammarström, A., Nilsson, K., Nordenmark, M., & Helen, R. (2012). Unemployment, gender and mental health: The roles of the gender regime. *Sociology of Health and Illness, 20*(10), 1–17.

Standing, G. (2014). The precarit: The new dangerous class. Bloomsbury.

Teo. T. (2009). Philosophical concerns in critical psychology. In D. Fox, I. Prilleltensky, & S. Austin (Eds.), *Critical Psychology: An introduction* (2nd edition) (pp. 36–54). SAGE.

Turban, D. B., Lee, F. K., Veiga, S. P. D. M., Haggard, D. L., & Wu, S. Y. (2013). Be happy, don't wait: The role of trait affect in job search. *Personnel Psychology, 66*(2), 483–514.

Wacker, A. (2012). The explanation of unemployment effects in the latent function model of Marie Jahoda – a critical assessment. In T. Kieselback & S. Mannila (Eds.), *Unemployment, Precarious Work and Health: Research and Policy Issues*. Springer.

Walkerdine, V., & Bansel, P. (2010). Neoliberalism, work and subjectivity: Towards a more complex account. *SAGE Handbook of Identities* (pp. 492–507). SAGE.

Walters, W. (2000). *Unemployment and government: Genealogies of the social*. University Press.

Walters, W. (2012). *Governmentality: Critical encounters*. Routledge.

Wanberg, C. R. (2012). The individual experience of unemployment. *Annual Review of Psychology, 63*, 369–396. Retrieved from https://pdfs.semanticscholar.org/5f51/a32fb7f6434bebeaf9169fb2bb3500d44cc6.pdf

Wood, A. J., & Burchell, B. J. (2018). Unemployment and wellbeing. In A. Lewis *Cambridge Handbook of Psychology and Economic Behaviour.* (2nd edition). (pp. 234–259). Cambridge University Press.

Yang, J. (2015). *Unknotting the heart: Unemployment and therapeutic governance in China.* Cornell University Press.

4

PARTICIPATION, ACTIVATION AND COMPLIANCE

Introduction

In this chapter, I want to highlight how we can denaturalise 'unemployment' by focusing on how unemployment is produced through policy-informed practices that claim to 'know' or 'solve' the problem of unemployment. Policy is often presented as a rational set of undertakings to solve a problem efficiently. The problems are positioned as exogenous to policy. For example, commenting on earlier iterations of Employment Services (ES) Ganley (2002) stated psychological understanding of the "*consequences* of joblessness" is integral to "mobilise societal commitment to *tackle* the problem" and to inform "policy *responses*" (p. 179, my emphasis). Here, studying policy as a 'response' leaves 'unemployment' and its 'effects' as self-evident and unproblematic. Tools such as critique, problematisation and governmentality allow researchers to re-examine practices and avoid (re) producing those very categories and practices that (re)shape unemployed subjectivities and lives.

As established in previous chapters, I start from the premise that unemployment is 'truthed' in many sites: such as statistical computations, media constructions of the 'dole bludger' and in the psychological literature as 'cause' or 'effect' of poor 'subjective wellbeing'. ES in Australia, currently called *jobactive,* is a key site where unemployment is 'truthed'. While our subjectivities are fluid and situation-dependent, a person 'serviced' within an ES provider ('provider') is treated first and foremost as 'unemployed'. To be marked out as experiencing unemployment requires a network of relations between "fields of knowledges" that are both drawn upon and created; "types of normativity" to be compared against, and technologies developed and deployed to constitute certain "forms of subjectivity" (Foucault, 1985, p. 6). In this way, ES is a site where a person *becomes* unemployed in and through disciplinary practices that (re)make ontological identities.

DOI: 10.4324/9781003112518-4

As I show later in this chapter, *jobactive* problematises unemployment via participation thus making 'participation' governmental through 'strengthening' mutual obligations (MO) and ensuring the unemployed comply in line with moral citizenship. Within policy-related documents,[1] I trace the 'making' and 'unmaking' (p. 69) of the unemployed subject. I followed Bacchi and Goodwin (2016, p. 20) by asking questions about how subject positions are implicated in representations of the 'problem' of unemployment, what assumptions underpin these representations, and the lived effects and silences that are then made possible. The problematisation approach helps to understand how specific versions of unemployment and the unemployed are made intelligible, with corresponding strategies of reformation, simultaneously making alternatives impossible, improbable or questionable. In the following sections, I follow the problem of 'participation' within *jobactive* and situate this 'urgent need' as a key function of the apparatus. I analyse discourses of activation, psy-complexified notions of 'wellbeing' and conditionality and discuss their underpinning power-knowledge relations. Through increasingly punitive activation and authoritarian governmentality, unemployment is solidified as an individual problem and the unemployed are produced as blameworthy.

The problematisation of ES: 'Helping' clients 'participate' in the workforce

In March 2015, then Prime Minister Tony Abbott announced that, from July, *jobactive* model of ES would replace Job Services Australia (JSA, 2009–2015). The announcement of the *jobactive* model situated the problem, and hence the justification for the policy move to *jobactive*, to be in the inherently 'flawed' JSA model. The main concern was providers had been unable to help clients gain and retain employment; they were "letting jobseekers down" hence the need to improve the "quality" of services by "investing $5 billion" (Abbott, 2015). Concerns outlined included "red tape" and "training for training's sake". These processes supposedly prohibited providers and their workers from "doing what they do best". The assumption here is that ES when functioning appropriately (i.e. as enabled through policy) *can* 'help' clients "find and keep a job".

This 'problem' of non-participation is also locatable in the problematisation of ES (rather than just *jobactive* specifically). The review into the welfare system, *A new system for better employment and social outcomes* ('welfare review') (Department of Social Services [DSS], 2015), stated its "purpose [was] to identify improvements to ensure the system is sustainable, effective and coherent, and encourages people to work" (p. 5). A policy cannot be generalised to 'all' people; the review panel was instructed to suggest strategies to improve the affordability, accessibility and efficiency of welfare policy as well as incentivise those "who can work" and support "those who are genuinely not able to work" (DSS, p. 6). To be an authentic and deserving welfare recipient here is to have a "severe disability" and consequently are "not *expected* to work". However, for everyone else, "there is an *expectation*" that "now or in the future" recipients "will be capable of some level of workforce participation" (DSS, p. 84, my emphasis).

Participation is a fundamental component of the *welfare review's* conception of the purpose of policy because it is 'expected' by 'society'. The *welfare review* claims that there is a "broad community acceptance" and expectation that "people who have the capacity to work should work where possible" (Department of Social Services, 2015, p. 62). 'Participation' in the workforce is not just an 'outcome' of policy but a social norm. 'Genuineness' acts as a statement that activates other moral discourses (Graham, 2011). It distinguishes those who can't and are excused, from those who can and are expected to participate in the labour force. Moral discourses around genuineness assume that everyone who is capable to do paid work has a duty to do so (Handler, 2003, p. 235). It also resonates with older Poor Law discourses about the unmotivated and undeserving poor (McGann et al., 2020). The need to ensure that people are 'participating' in the workforce is connected to the welfare review's position that the 'current' welfare system is "failing to identify groups at risk of long-term income support dependence" (DSS, p. 9) and so needs to "invest" in evidence-based 'early-intervention' strategies that will boost 'employability' to improve 'participation'.

A running objective that links each document discussed above is the need to ensure welfare recipients are 'participating' in some way. The focus of governmental intervention is primarily located on the bodies and minds of the unemployed. This turn to 'supply-side' intervention over demand management approaches (such as full employment objectives, for example) is part of a larger trend in OECD member countries. In the next section, I sketch a brief historical and international context to outline these changes before returning to the case study to pull out examples of how such neoliberal political rationalities manifest in and through the welfare-work nexus in contemporary Australia.

The emergence of activation as *a remedy*

The importance of the 'need' to 'activate' is integral to how 'participation' is conceptualised in *jobactive* and ES. 'Activation' is a key epistemological assumption underpinning policies that steer the unemployed to 'participate' in a pre-established 'right' way. The point of activation practices is to motivate the unemployed to 'actively' find work (Department of Employment [DE], 2015a; Organisation for Economic Cooperation and Development [OECD], 2012; Sage, 2013). Indeed, in Australian welfare practices the idea that the unemployed 'need' to be 'activated' is positioned as indisputable as the *welfare review* claims "activation works" (Department of Social Services, 2015, p. 6). Such 'common sense' notions about activation tend to ignore research questioning the 'effectiveness' of activation to show that 'active' labour market programs have produced mixed results (Brodkin & Marston, 2013; Frings-Sen et al., 2010; Sage, 2019). Nevertheless, I do not want to discuss whether 'activation works' but how 'activation' is constituted as the solution.

The turn to the 'active society' and 'activation' strategies to reduce unemployment has underpinned policy contexts in many Western countries since the mid-1990s (Moreira & Lødemel, 2014). As part of this shift, individuals and their behaviour (supply) became the target of policy. There is less will to intervene in the market to improve demand by employer groups. In this landscape, activation strategies keep the unemployed attached to the labour market, ensuring there is a surplus of motivated and job-ready labour (Immervoll & Scarpetta, 2012; Pinto, 2019; Wong & Au-Yeong, 2018). Activation implies a move away from what has been positioned as 'passive' forms of welfare to one that attempts to reconstruct the unemployed person through activities such as job search, vocational training, positive psychology programs, non-vocational skills (effective communication, presentations), job interview skills and motivation training among others.

The policy turn to foreground supply-side intervention of unemployment is traceable in OECD documents. As an international body, the OECD exercises normative governance through recommendations on how to govern the unemployed. At the end of the 1980s, there was growing concern that improvements in the general economy, recessionary events (notably the 1970s oil crisis) and falling unemployment were insufficient: "the tide was not raising all ships" (OECD, 2012, p. 7). The problem of unemployment moved away from demand side considerations to focus on labour-market mismatch or structural unemployment. Policy interventions came to be concerned with addressing long-term unemployment and the risk of removing welfare dependency. While some envisioned the active society would provide opportunities for active engagement in society over their life course including education, volunteering and care work (Gass, 1988), the OECD focused on promoting a welfare state that "enable[d]" people to participate actively in society, *and in particular in the labour market*" (1990, p. ix, my emphasis). Accordingly, policy norms aligned the solution to unemployment with the process of defining and measuring unemployment. In line with the International Labour Organisation's (ILO) definition of unemployment, job search is only counted as such if it involved, "active contact with a potential employer to apply for a job, and includes a contact by phone or in person, by submitting a written application, or by attending a job interview" (Department of Employment, 2015a, p. 61). The focus on an active society also requires differentiating 'active' from what it is not. Activation discourses thus constituted a 'former' welfare state that "merely" providing income support as 'passive' (OECD, 1990, p. ix). The solution to passivity has been the creation of a welfare landscape that provides a programmatic focus on activities, and thereby also creates a set of behaviours that can be observed, measured and compared. In some OECD countries, there was a second wave of reforms in the 2010s that saw some countries incorporate privatisation into their service delivery. Australia has been at the forefront of quasi-marketised approaches that individualise unemployment.

Alongside these changes was a connected discourse of 'pathological' unemployment. Positioning the 'passive' welfare state as the key problem, US-based scholars such as Charles Murray and Lawrence Mead advocated for 'workfare' and conditional welfare to incite the unemployed to look for work. The 'need' to keep the unemployed job searching and improving their 'job readiness' relies on the assumption that the unemployed will become idle and demoralised and so, for their benefit, need to be 'employed' in some activity. This 'pathological' theory of unemployment stems from influential ideas about the unemployed lacking key psychological traits and affectivity, such as motivation, self-efficacy and self-esteem, which are all preventable (Mead, 1997). These afflictions are remedied through paternalistic welfare or creating the conditions to steer conduct, or in the words of a former Minister for Employment, "hassle to help" (cited in Fowkes, 2011) the unemployed back into employment. These ideas underpin workfare regimes in the United Kingdom, United States, and New Zealand/ Aotearoa. In Australia as in other countries, these ideas have been connected to continued efforts since the mid-1990s to ensure welfare recipients do not malinger on welfare and become 'dependent' (Mestan, 2014). In the next section, I show how activation is the core discursive practice of ES – *jobactive* – that obliges clients to 'participate'.

Activating the unemployed through 'mutual obligations' (MO)

In this section, I focus on a specific policy practice, 'MO', to excavate the 'problem' of 'participation' I start with the premise that what we decide to do about a 'problem' is indicative of what we think needs to change. I return to the theme of how 'participation' is underpinned by 'activation' discourses. I discuss how clients are being punished for failure to participate *appropriately*. It is the nature of 'punishment' rather than the 'need' to 'activate' that is rendered questionable in the broader public debate about the 'purpose' of *jobactive*. Effectively, the 'problem' of participation is now so entrenched as 'common sense' that 'activation' and 'MO' are rarely questioned. Unsettling *how* participation comes to be the problem, therefore, is part of the critical work of this book to think differently about unemployment.

We can trace National unemployment benefits started in Australia in the mid 1940s. We can identify continuities and discontinuities between the original scheme and the current model *jobactive*. These changes follow shifting ideas and assumptions about ES, the role of the market, and State intervention into society. In the pre-war years, unemployment benefits were designed on the premise that 'unemployment' was a problem of macroeconomics. At that time, there was an assumption that the demand would be set by the market and jobs would materialise. For example, such presumptions were made explicit in the Harvester Judgement that established a living wage and as such prioritised not only a (white) male's wages as a breadwinner but also assumed job demand would be assured by the market (O'Donnell, 2019). However, it was also assumed that the Government could and should intervene in the market to stimulate demand. So much so that pursuing full employment was Government policy (Commonwealth of Australia white papers, 1945 as cited in Coombs, 1994). These core assumptions remained for the next few decades, and it was not until the 1980s that substantial changes to unemployment benefits coincided with a major shift in the underlying assumptions.

The unemployment benefit scheme was mostly unaltered from 1945 until the mid-1970s. The 1980s saw significant changes in how best to 'deal' with this 'problem'. Unemployment benefits were always conditional but with the 'active employment strategy' a slightly different rationale for conditionality for the design, and allocation of unemployment emerged. In the 'active employment strategy', the unemployed had to satisfy the 'activity test' instead of the 'work test' (Ey, 2012). The 'work test' allowed the Director-General to cancel the payment of an unemployment benefit if the recipient was voluntarily unemployed "without good and sufficient reason", was unemployed due to misconduct or had "refused or failed, without good and sufficient reason, to accept an office of employment which the Director-General considers to be suitable" (Commonwealth of Australia, 1945, Section 28). As O'Donnell (2019) pointed out the 1945 legislation broke with trade union pre-war out-of-work schemes that would provide support for members to delay employment until they found work that suited their current occupation or trade. The 'work test' prioritised getting any reasonable job over getting a specific trade-appropriate job. The 'work test' demonstrates how unemployment was constituted as *involuntary* and temporary.

From the 1980s 'unemployment' came to be regarded as a problem of the individual rather than lack of demand for workers. By the end of the decade, unemployment was high after three decades of trending at 2% (it was not until the 1970s that unemployment started heading towards 6%). Factors that are often put forward to explain the increase in unemployment include changes in the structure of the Australian economy, such as the decline of manufacturing, offshoring of production or the increased presence of women in the labour market. Full employment was no longer a policy aim (Coombs, 1994). According to the social security review, the '*Cass Review*' (Cass et al., 1988), this economic backdrop meant the 'work test' "became [a] meaningless activity". It was meaningless because "the likelihood of a positive outcome [was] low" and therefore it was assumed that it also did nothing to fix the supposed incongruence between the skills of labour and the skills required by the market (structural unemployment).

The *Cass Review* was influential on welfare policy and ensuring clients take 'active steps' became central to welfare 'service' provision. This shift in Australian welfare policy was contingent on other trends in political and economic thought that were (and still are) occupying policy discussions both in Australia and in other countries of the Global North. Indeed, the *Cass Review* mirrored the OECD (1990) concern that a 'passive welfare state' renders people 'demoralised', 'dependent' and accordingly increases social exclusion. The solution was 'active society' and 'activation', which was premised on leaving the market to its own devices (and not pursuing full employment) (Dean, 2006). Evidence relating to demand side considerations was ignored and individual explanations for unemployment were deemed to be the most satisfactory (Cook, 2005). As already mentioned, commentators in countries such as the United States were arguing that the welfare state was part of the problem by its provision of benefits, and through a focus on external factors. It was argued that what was required was individual behavioural change (Mead, 1986). In line with these international changes, Australian welfare provision in the 1990s became oriented towards 'workfare' by focusing on discourses of 'work-first' and activation.

Activation is operationalised through the Deed – the contract that outlines a framework for what is allowed to be 'done' to, with and for, clients. The Deed outlines the 'practicalities' of activating. Activation is enforced through 'MO' or the "tasks and activities you agree to do, to help you find a job" (Services Australia, 2021). To receive their fortnightly payments clients, need to demonstrate that they complete the activities listed in their agreement with their provider (the 'Job Plan'), go to their provider appointments, complete and report their job searches (up to 20 a month), and accept any offer of suitable paid work (Services Australia, 2021). Job Plan activities can include WfD (Work for Dole), volunteering, education or training in vocational or non-vocational programs or activities that are "designed to reduce [labour market] disadvantage" (Services Australia). These can include mental health counselling or rehabilitation. Job Plans are supposed to be updated at every appointment to ensure they reflect the client's current situation and appointments with providers are supposed to be monthly although providers can request more frequent appointments.

Providers must "actively monitor" clients' to "ensure jobseekers remain active and engaged *while* looking for work" (Department of Employment, 2015b, p. 113, my emphasis). In this way, enforcing 'participation' is more than ensuring clients look for jobs but also *attend* appointments, *enter* into a Job Plan, *fulfil* their annual activity requirement (such as WfD) or other compulsory activity (as specified in the Job Plan). Being 'active' here is operationalised into behaviours that can be observed, monitored and enforced. As I will go on to discuss, breaking participation and activation into these governable micro-practices is legitimised through the *Social Security Act*, but also through 'regimes of truth'. The unemployed *should* attend appointments with their provider because it is assumed they 'need' to be 'activated', they 'should' be activated, the provider has the skill set to activate, and non-compliance is a direct violation of responsible citizenship. These assumptions legitimate increasing punitive activation strategies. In what follows, I look at the practice of 'MO' and how it connects 'activation' with 'citizenship' and how they have been produced, defended and disseminated.

Merging discourses of 'activation' with moral citizenship

The concept of 'MO', introduced into the policy sphere via the *Participation Support for a more equitable Australia: Final Report* (McClure, 2000) and was materialised under Job Network, widened the space for privatisation and quasi-marketisation of ES. In 1998 the privatised 'Job Network' replaced the public Commonwealth ES (CES, Senate, 2009). Job Network rested on the rationale that exposing ES to a competitive market space would improve the quality of services and outcomes as well as increase choice for clients (Productivity Commission, 2002). The changes to ES, therefore, were in line with international changes referred to as 'New Public Management' an ensemble of ideas drawn from the private sector to reduce costs and improve efficiency (Considine et al., 2018). 'MO' was based on the idea that the unemployed have responsibilities to fulfil in return for the receipt of social security (Department of Employment, 2015b, p. 11). This included actively looking for work, and improving their job competitiveness as well as "give[ing] something back to the community that supports them" (Yeend, 2004, para. 3). In effect, providers were contracted to enforce compliance and ensure that the unemployed are 'participating' as 'good citizens'.

In addition to 'fairness', the idea of MO is presented as the unemployed 'giving back' to society. The implicit idea here is that citizens enter into a 'social contract' that stipulates a reciprocal relationship between the citizen and the state. To be considered a 'good' citizen, the subject must embody the principles of activeness, responsibility and individual autonomy. They are expected to demonstrate and become the ideal, unemployed subject. According to the tenets of neoliberalism "those who refuse to become responsible and govern themselves ethically have also refused the offer to become members of our moral community" (Rose, 2000, p. 1407, see also Mead, 1986). Here clients are divided from 'taxpayers' and distinguished as refusing moral citizenship through labour market participation. As will be discussed in more detail below, failure to comply with the 'moral' worker-citizen discourse is punishable by measures that may have a substantial impact on the subject and the lives they can live.

The idea that welfare recipients have 'obligations' in order to receive income support was not entirely novel. Both the *Cass Review* and the 1994 *Working Nation* White paper on unemployment discussed a similar concept, 'reciprocal obligations'. Harris (2001) maintained that there are similarities and differences between the 'mutual' and 'reciprocal' obligations. He suggested that the *Working Nation* paper and the *Cass Review* did not challenge the view that, as citizens, the unemployed were 'entitled' to support from the State. Harris suggests that with the privatisation of ES in 1998, the state's responsibility to support the unemployed started to diminish. Indeed, critics of the privatisation of ES have noted that the structure of contractual arrangements lacks transparency with clauses such as 'commercial-in-confidence', undermining the possibility to hold the state and provider organisations accountable (see Farrow et al., 2015).

Conditionality by way of accepting 'suitable' job offers has always been a part of a Commonwealth unemployment benefit scheme (as I mentioned above). However, with the changing responsibilities and commitments of the neoliberal state, accepting a job offer placed a moral burden on the unemployed. MO declared that it was only "fair that clients take up reasonable offers of employment" (DEET, 1992, p. 21, as cited in Harris, 2001). MO seem to only apply to clients, and not to the State to improve demand or to employers. The onus is on clients to be productive and contribute has been likened to a type of "luck egalitarianism", compliance with obligations demonstrating they are the "deserving poor" (White, 2004). To refuse or resist shows they are voluntarily poor and open to blame (McGann et al., 2020). In this way, the main problematisation hides some of the other issues with finding a job. For example, ageism, ableism, (Australian Human Rights Commission, 2016) and racism (Carangio et al., 2020) are problems affecting hiring practices in Australia. Still, the policy maintains that if you are *actively* looking for a job then you should find one. As a consequence, the unemployed are not just 'passive' but 'deficit'. The unemployed are assumed to be lacking the vital characteristics that are otherwise present in the working population. The purpose of ES provision in Australia shifted from constituting unemployment from involuntary to voluntary; activation discourses *produce* the passive, demoralised and unconfident subject as the problem to be tackled by policy. As I will discuss, failure to find or accept a job incurred financial penalties. This move to authoritarian governmentality relies on the assumptions that people who do not have a job choose to do so, and therefore, it is 'reasonable' for the State to blame and punish them.

'Strengthening' MO by punishing non-participation

The introduction of *jobactive* is a key moment to locate how the logics of activation intersect with moral discourses and technologies to legitimatise punishing clients for not participating in the market. Indeed, the changes to the ES model via the introduction of *jobactive* occurred alongside automated processes to penalise clients for not attending appointments and promises by politicians to 'strengthen' MO through legislation and punish the non-compliant.

There were three changes made with *jobactive* to ensure clients complied with their MO to attend and participate. This three-step process included the Non-Attendance Report (NAR) (which was introduced in the later part of 2014), 'suspend till attend' policy (which was introduced in early 2015) and the alterations to the participation report (that became active in July 2015 with the start of *jobactive*). The NAR was an automatic suspension of a payment initiated when providers reported a client to the state (via Centrelink) for not attending an appointment. The 'suspend until attend' policy meant income suspension until the client attended a 'reengagement' appointment. Finally, the 'provider appointment report' (part of the participation report) allowed providers to recommend clients incur a financial penalty for non-attendance or "inappropriate" behaviour at appointment or another MO activity (such as WfD) (DE, n.d.). "Strengthening MO" was operationalised by increasing the potential to penalise clients. This included trying to remove 'waivers' for these penalties like with the 'serious failures' charge.

Removing the waiver for a serious penalty was a failed attempt to widen the scope to penalise clients. 'Serious failures' included persistent non-compliance with participation obligations or not accepting an offer of suitable employment, and not coming to appointments or completing adequate job search. The penalty for 'serious failures' was a loss of 8 weeks income. However, this penalty could be waived if it was deemed that the client was experiencing financial hardship or if the client selected to complete an alternative activity (such as work experience or WfD, approved training or intensive job search) (Commonwealth of Australia, 1991, p. 42). This waiver was implemented under JSA to reduce the severity of financial penalties for vulnerable clients (Thomas, 2014). Such concerns included the risk that already disadvantaged clients would disengage from the labour market, as well as the possible additional demands placed on health, housing and justice sectors as well as other community services (DEEWR, 2010).

The *Social Security Amendment (Stronger Penalties for Serious Failures) Bill* ('Stronger Penalties') (Commonwealth of Australia, 2014, p. 11) proposed to remove the waiver for clients who refuse work and only allow persistent non-compliant clients one opportunity to waive the 8-week penalty. 'Stronger Penalties' was justified on the ground that it is a 'human right to work' and that the Bill "encourages" clients to "engage with their right to work by providing a stronger incentive to accept an offer of suitable work". In doing so "more clients experience the benefits of employment" such as "social and economic inclusions". Moreover, the Bill was presented as complying with the 'right to work' in terms of the right to choose what sort of work, since incurring serious penalty suggests "the person is employable, and they are likely to have other choices as to what work they do" (Parliament of Australia, 2014, p. 11). These changes were presented as 'needed' because the procedure at the time (opportunity to waive penalties and reinstate payments at reconnecting appointments) failed to incentivise clients to comply with their MO (Thomas, 2018).

At a discursive level, the proposed removal of the waiver would "uphold the fundamental principle that taxpayer-funded income support payments are provided as a safety net" for people who are "genuine", and they are not "an option for people who have been offered a job but simply refuse to work" (Department of Employment, 2015b, p. 9). Indeed, the option of a waiver is presented as an "insufficient deterrent to refusing work" (Thomas, 2018, para. 4). The distinction made between 'genuine' clients and those who are choosing not to work is reinforced through the Government using social media to advocate for removing the waiver (see Figure 4.1). Here, those clients who 'simply refuse' to work are regarded as 'welfare cheats'. When positioning the unemployed, or a segment of unemployed, as deliberately defying the rules of MO, there is also the suggestion 'welfare cheats' are rejecting their implicit agreements under the social contract. The implication that people are choosing not to work justifies increasing punitive measures of activation. However, it is also an example of the 'emotional' component of policy where the subjects of policy are supposed to 'feel' a certain way. In the spaces of ES, *jobactive* policy involves governing the unemployed to ensure they 'feel' motivated to constitute job searching as I discuss later in this chapter (and in Chapter Five). Here, however, social media campaigns show how 'emotions' are part of the arsenal to mark out and publicly shame clients who refuse to participate as moral members of society.

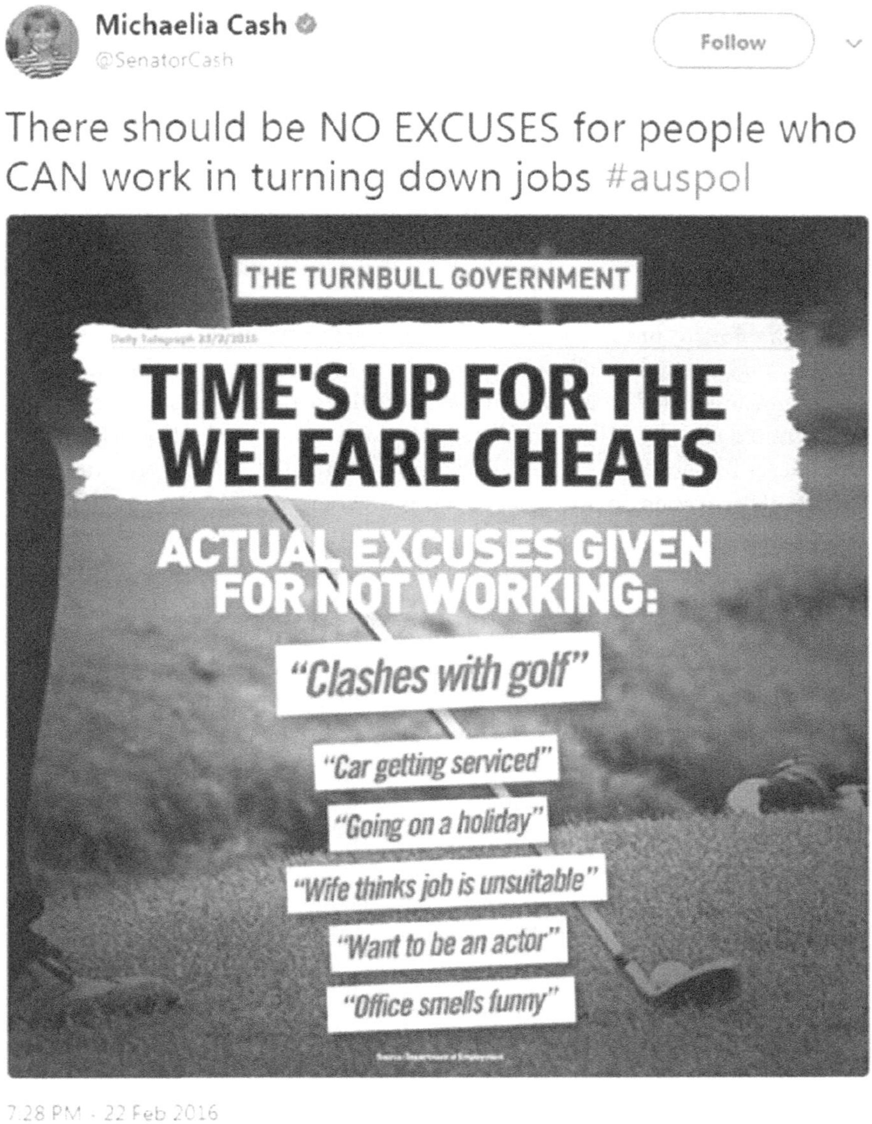

FIGURE 4.1 Former Minister for Employment M. Cash expressing her concern on social media about job seekers not taking up 'suitable employment'.

This 'stronger' approach to disciplining the unemployed is in stark contrast to the recommendations from the *welfare review*. The *review* presented MO as "one of a range of tools" that should be wielded by service providers (although it is the Department of Human Services, via Centrelink, that actually enforces MO through sanctions) to "tailor an individual's support package" (Department of Social Services, 2015, p. 132).

Increasing conditionality

Despite concern about the harmful impact of conditionality and welfare activation – stigma, demoralisation, self-blame and entrenched poverty (McGann et al., 2020; Peterie et al., 2019; O'Halloran et al., 2020) – conditionality has steadily increased. The will to 'strengthen' conditionality persists and follows an international trend of increasing punitive and coercive welfare practices in other Anglophone OECD member countries such as Ireland, the United Kingdom and the United States (Dukelow & Kennett, 2018; Mestan, 2014; Wright & Patrick, 2019). Two notable examples in Australia are 'Robo Debt' and Income management (IM).

In an effort to further cut red tape and improve the efficiency of the welfare system, and encourage clients to comply and not commit welfare fraud, the government initiated an automated data-matching system to locate overpayments (Morrison & Porter, 2016). The system was found to be methodologically flawed and illegal by the High Court (Henriques-Gomes, 2020). Another extreme example of 'activation' practices, compulsory income management (CIM) 'quarantines' certain clients' income on-premises that clients need 'help' to manage their finances and curtail alcohol consumption (Staines et al., 2020). These paternalistic practices do little to achieve their stated outcomes and instead infantilise and further impoverish the already disadvantaged (Mendes et al., 2020).

But even looking at the most mundane of practices demonstrates how entrenched activation and welfare conditionality is in the Australian welfare regime. In July 2018 the government managed to sidestep the problem of wavering penalties by implementing the Targeted Compliance Framework (TCF). Clients start in the green zone and accumulate demerit points for non-compliance. From July to December 2018 42.5% of the *jobactive* caseload had accrued 1 demerit point (a measure for non-compliance), which resulted in a payment suspension (Senate, 2019). The process still involves automated payment suspensions for non-attendance at an activity or appointment. To be moved into the 'penalty zone', clients are first assessed to ensure that compliance activities were appropriate for their situation. In effect, the rearranging of penalty applications means that penalties cannot be 'waived' (Services Australia, 2021) but there is a "compliance assessment" before a client moves into the penalty zone to ensure that the client's MO were "reasonable" for their circumstances (Services Australia 2021).

Continuing on from concerns about the 'need' to strengthen compliance the TCF continues to remove opportunities for discretion and human intervention (McGann et al., 2020). Enforcement of MO has been contracted to providers that are incentivised to meet key performance indicators to increase revenue. As argued by Bredgaard and Larson (2007) incentivising private organisations to find "the quickest route possible" (p. 294) to (re)employ clients makes it easier to implement welfare conditionality than is possible in the public sector. But it also raises issues about how these punitive activation practices impact people's lives, especially considering the inadequate level of the income support and the impact a suspension will have on people's ability to meet their basic needs (Senate, 2019).

The combination of insufficient income support and punitive activation shows how the current Australian welfare state is designed to punish the poor (Parsell et al., 2021). Affect and psy technologies are integral to this end, particularly in using shame and disgust through regimes of deterrence that have uneven implications for welfare recipients (Mills & Klein, 2021). The practices of jobactive produces different unemployed subjects, but these discourses sit alongside one another in the daily practices of activation. In the next section I focus on another unemployed subjectivity: the despairing subject.

(Let) down and (missing) out: The despairing and disadvantaged client

This final section will focus on the people who are central to the problematisation of unemployed: the unemployed. The practices of policy produce a certain subject, and in *jobactive* policy, the 'unemployed' is produced as a 'problem'. Hence, a 'solution' to the 'problem' of the 'unemployed' is made both 'simple' and 'necessary'. In this way, *jobactive* policy both 'makes' and 'unmakes' the unemployed subject (Bacchi & Goodwin, 2016). In other words, starting with the 'problem' of the non/participating subject, we can trace processes involved in 'becoming-other' via the 'lines of subjectification' (Deleuze, 1992). These processes open possibilities for what kind of subject it is possible to become and not a 'guarantee' of individual self-governing practices. Yet, they are still important to study since *jobactive* governing practices shape the 'modes of existence' and set the 'rules of the game' for intervention practices. I focus in this section on case management and how it produces the 'despairing subject', a line of inquiry that will be revisited in the next chapter.

Case management is key to understanding the now 'common sense' approach of 'activation' that informs ES (Van Berkel & Van der Aa, 2012). Case management is constituted of personal interactions resting on the idea that workers can motivate the unemployed to look for work and self-govern to improve employability. The problem of the unemployed as dangerously discouraged clients is placed at the centre of case management practices, rendering the unemployed 'deficit' and in 'need' of 'psy-informed' 'help'. Such practices rely on Jahoda's (1982) legacy in the psychology of unemployment literature, arguing that unemployment deprives people of the benefits of employment.

The *jobactive* deed provides the 'rules of the game' for providers to organise their spaces, develop 'innovative' service delivery programs and use discretion to attune these practices to individual 'needs'. The outsourcing of ES was envisioned as allowing providers the flexibility and discretion to "pursue more innovative problems faced by jobseekers in securing employment" (Department for Employment, Education & Welfare Relations, DEEWR, sub 43, p. 18, as cited in Productivity Commission, 2002, p. 3.8). Employment Consultants can use 'discretion' to take into consideration the mitigating circumstances of the client and the realities of the local labour market (Department of Employment, 2015a). *Jobactive,* as spelt out in the *Employment Service Guarantee,* should provide clients with individualised servicing and, in terms of subjectification, individualise clients since the focus is on identifying personalised 'needs' and 'wants'.

The verbs used in the *Employment Services Guarantee* highlight who defines these needs. The consultants define the 'needs', 'strengths', 'matching' and 'referring'. Workers here are produced as certain types of experts in being able to do such 'defining'. Clients, on the other hand, have to do 'everything [they] have agreed to do' – complete activities and so forth. They have to 'make every effort' (activity test) and 'accept any (suitable) job offer' (work test). Discursively, clients are only allowed 'agency' if that means looking for work.

The imperative to incorporate clients' 'needs' and 'goals' into service delivery is not novel to *jobactive* and indeed was a component in previous policy initiatives including Working Nation, Job Network and JSA (Fowkes, 2011). Across time, evaluations of ES have lamented the lack of individually tailored practices and repeatedly recommend increased focus on improving the individualised aspect of case management (APESAA, 2012; Senate, 2019). Indeed, research argued that ES runs a "two-speed nature of outcomes": one that provides "adequate results" for those frictionally unemployed or who are job ready and transiting between jobs but chronically underperformed" with helping "complex critical cases of disadvantage". Indeed this "failure" to 'help' the disadvantaged "appears entrenched" (Farrow et al., 2015, p. 25).

Effective case management requires employment consultants to be suitably qualified. Here an embedded problematisation (Bacchi & Goodwin, 2016) of employment consultants as authorities highlights how the unemployed are problematised as *psychological* and *emotional* subjects. Research has noted that workers rely on personal experience and other areas of informal expertise to perform case management since workers in ES do not tend to come from social work or other psy backgrounds (McDonald & Marston, 2005). Research suggests qualifications among consultants is not only "disturbingly low" but the few with tertiary education have qualifications (20%) "unrelated to ES, social work or psychology", raising the likelihood that workers will not have the appropriate theoretical tools to do their job appropriately (Jobs Australia, 2012, p. 8; Senate, 2019). The *welfare review* (Department of Social Services, 2015) advocated for an 'investment approach' based on a 'warp-around approach' that built individualised capacity. These individualised approaches assume that personalised services ensure the unemployed feels they have been heard and feel 'empowered', potentially softening the punitive aspects of activation (Casey, 2020; Neville, 2013) but whether these are actually realisable is contested (see Chapter Five).

The *jobactive* apparatus intersects with the 'psy-complex' in contemporary problematisations about unemployment and ES via activation. Accordingly, to deny, or at least not to 'help' people 'participate' in the marketplace, leaves them disadvantaged and 'missing out' on the taken-for-granted benefits of work. As I discussed earlier, part of the need to move towards behavioural focus with the unemployed in the 1980s was connected to psy-complexified ideas around the 'economic' issue that the unemployed can become 'discouraged' and 'detached' from the labour market. Being 'discouraged', however, assumes that the subject has suffered the effects of being unemployed and from this despair, has stopped actively looking for work. Dean (1995) noted that this problem of the 'discouraged' individual was reconfigured into a lack, namely of 'job readiness' and the 'risk of welfare dependency'. The first issue relates to the failure to re-enter the labour market because a person lacks the skills, attitudes and motivation to do so and the second refers to the risk of becoming solely dependent on social security for extended periods. The danger about the discouraged subject is they risk becoming the welfare-dependent subject. The very opposite of the "self-reliant" (Department of Social Services, 2015, p. 9) (neoliberal) subject that welfare policy should 'support'.

In the *announcement of jobactive* 'work-first' discourses held together assumptions about individuals, citizenship, work and 'wellbeing'. The *announcement* suggested JSA was "letting jobseekers down". This 'problem' was being 'solved' by *jobactive* through prioritising 'work-first'. This made it possible to 'say', within the 'true' that "the best form of welfare is a job" (Abbott, 2015, para. 7). 'Welfare' here is a pun: it refers to the 'welfare state' and the 'wellbeing' of a group. The work-first discourse extends beyond citizenship by also merging 'welfare', as in "wellbeing", with 'work'. As it is framed, (re)employment should be prioritised by policy because it would be immoral to deny citizens these benefits. Governing, especially in the neoliberal frame, is about ensuring the wellbeing and optimisation of a population (Foucault, 2008). Quick re-employment (avoiding long-term unemployment) is a priority for governing the unemployed to avoid the issues with 'depending' on welfare. Indeed, other problems are deprioritised since 'work' should come 'first'.

In the case of mental ill-health, for example, the *welfare review* (Department of Social Services, 2015, p. 20) specifically outlines how (re)employment can be part of the "recovery plan" for people with "lived experience of mental health conditions" because "being able to secure a job and contribute in a workplace are important normalising milestones". Discursively, the dividing practice of 'normal/abnormal' segregates 'employed/unemployed' and 'mental health/mental ill-health' along similar lines. That is, 'normality' as produced through work helps to alleviate 'mental health conditions'; to not do so leaves someone at a disadvantage. The review does acknowledge that such 'normalising' needs a "healthy work environment" to provide 'optimal' 'health benefits' (p. 61) although work-first discourses prioritise 'any job', over a 'good job' (Marston et al., 2019). Work is ideal 'welfare' because within this discourse, work has a therapeutic function. With the intersection of psy and the *jobactive* apparatuses, activation also becomes about ensuring the 'wellbeing' of the population through economic participation, facilitated through personalised case management. Discursively, it becomes dangerous for unemployed subjects to resist subjectification and 'desire' to become something other than a worker-citizen. I suggest it becomes almost impossible *not* to want to 'participate' in society through work because to do so is irresponsibly putting one's own 'wellbeing' at risk.

Concluding comments

Policy documents, contracts and guidelines, welfare reviews, and media releases of *jobactive* offer a way of researching the 'problem' *jobactive* was assembled to 'solve'.

Part of this chapter's objective was to contextualise *jobactive* and its strategies and technologies of intervention through administrative procedures and frameworks that establish the 'rules of the game' to inform providers' governing practices. Unemployment is not 'out there' ready for policy to address and rectify but actively constructed through policy. I have highlighted how the very notion of individualised services or activation relied on psy-complexified notions of an individual who, in not being 'active', is assumed to be 'passive'. In assuming unemployment is voluntary, the internal processes of the unemployed individual – their thoughts, affects/feelings/emotions and attitudes – become the site of reformation over and above and demand-focused solutions to unemployment. In the next chapter, I trace such discourses through interviews and operations with an ES provider to map a topographical account of governing the unemployed. I take a post-disciplinary approach that draws on critical psychological and post-Foucauldian insights to challenge the psy-complexified notions of 'unemployment' and to think critically about research practices and the objects/subjects produced therein. Thus, connecting this chapter to the overarching objectives of the book, to untangle and disrupt the taken-for-granted assumptions about unemployment and move beyond blaming the unemployed.

Note

1 Documents include practical texts that inform the framework and/or rationale around *jobactive* and welfare policy. These include the *jobactive* Deed ('the Deed') (the contract between the Australian Government and Employment Service Providers), media releases, Hansard documents, 2015 welfare review (Department of Social Services, 2015), and since the Deed is written in 'legalese' I also studied the documents that 'translate' the Deed into 'laypeople terms' and which are relied upon by workers to interpret the Deed such as *jobactive* factsheets/practical guidelines.

References

Abbott, T. (2015). *New jobactive service to help more jobseekers into work.* (Press release) Retrieved from https://www.pm.gov.au/media/2015-03-31/new-jobactive-services-help-more-jobseekers-work.

Abramovitz, M. (2006). Welfare reform in the United States: Gender, race and class matter. *Critical Social Policy, 26*(2), 336–364.

Advisory Panel on Employment Services Administration and Accountability (APESAA). (2012, November 12). Final report. Australian Government. Retrieved from https://docs.employment.gov.au/node/4238.

Australian Human Rights Commission (AHRC). (2016). Willing to work: National Inquiry into employment discrimination against older Australians and Australians with a disability. AHRC. Retrieved from https://humanrights.gov.au/our-work/age-discrimination/publications/willing-work-national-inquiry-employment-discrimination

Bacchi, C., & Goodwin, S. (2016). *Poststructural policy analysis: A guide to practice.* Palgrave Macmillan.

Bredgaard, T., & Larsen, F. (2007). Implementing public policy: What happens when non-public agencies take over? *International Journal of Sociology and Social Policy, 27*(7/8), 287–300.

Brodkin, E. Z., & Marston, G. (Eds.). (2013). *Work and the Welfare State: Street level organizations and workfare politics*. Georgetown University Press.

Carangio, V., Farquharson, K., Bertone, S., & Rajendran, D. (2020). Racism and White privilege: highly skilled immigrant women workers in Australia. *Ethnic and Racial Studies, 44*, 77–96. 10.1080/01419870.2020.1722195

Casey, S. (2020). *Mutual obligations after COVID-19: The work for the dole timebomb*. Per Capita Discussion Paper. Per Captia.

Cass, B., Gibson, F., & Tito, F. (1988). *Towards enabling policies: Income support for people with disabilities* (Social security review. Issues paper; no. 5). Australian government.

Commonwealth of Australia. (1945). Unemployment and Sickness Benefits Ac [C1944A00010]. Retrieved from https://www.legislation.gov.au/Details/C1944A00010.

Commonwealth of Australia. (1991). Social Security Act [C2013C00081]. Retrieved from http://www.austlii.edu.au/au/legis/cth/consol_act/ssa1991186/

Commonwealth of Australia. (2014). Social Security Legislation Amendment (Stronger penalties for serious failures) Bill 2014. Retrieved from https://www.legislation.gov.au/Details/C2014B00120/Explanatory%20Memorandum/Text.

Considine, M., Nguyen, P., & O'Sullivan, S. (2018). New public management and the rule of economic incentives: Australian welfare-to-work from job market signalling perspective. *Public Management Review, 20*(8), 1186–1204.

Cook, B. (2005). Welfare 'Reform' in Australia, 1975 to 2004: From entitlement to obligation. Retrieved from http://www.basicincome.qut.edu.au/documents/Beth per cent20Cook per cent20Coffee per cent20Paper per cent202004 per cent20for per cent20Biga.pdf.

Coombs, H. C. (1994). *From Curtin to Keating: The 1945 and 1994 white papers on employment: A better environment for human and economic diversity?: A discussion paper*. Australian National University.

Dean, M. (1995). Governing the unemployed self in an active society. *Economy and Society, 24*(4), 559–583. 10.1080/03085149500000025

Dean, M. (2006). Governmentality and the powers of life and death. In G. Marston & C. McDonald (Eds.), *Analysing Social Policy: A Governmental Approach*. Edward Elgar Publishing Limited.

Deleuze, G. (1992). What is a dispositif? In T. Armstrong (Ed.), *Michel Foucault, Philosopher: Essays*. Harvester Wheatsheaf.

Department of Education, Employment and Workplace Relations (DEEWR). (2010). Submission to the Independent review into the impact of the jobseeker compliance framework. Retrieved from http://parlinfo.aph.gov.au/parlInfo/search/display/display.w3p;query=Id%3A%22library%2Fjrnart%2F3349937%22

Department of Employment (DE) (n.d.). *Appendix B.6 Employment*. Retrieved from https://www.cuttingredtape.gov.au/sites/default/files/files/B_6_Employment.pdf

Department of Employment. (2015a). Jobactive Deed 2015–2020. Accessed 25 September 2015 from https://docs.employment.gov.au/documents/final-jobactive-deed-2015–2020.

Department of Employment. (2015b). Jobactive Factsheet. Retrieved from https://www.dese.gov.au/download/6131/program-fact-sheet-jobactive/9413/document/docx

Department of Social Services (2015). A new system for Better Employment and Social Outcomes: Report of the reference group on welfare reform to the Minister for Social Services. Canberra: Department of Employment. Retrieved from https://www.dss.gov.au/review-of-australias-welfare-system/a-new-system-for-better-employment-and-social-outcomes-full-version-of-the-final-report.

Dukelow, F., & Kennett, P. (2018). Discipline, debt and coercive commodification: Post-crisis neoliberalism and the welfare state in Ireland, the UK and the USA. *Critical Social Policy, 38*(3), 482–504. 10.1177/0261018318762727

Ey, C. (2012, December 4). *Social security payments for the unemployed, the sick and those in special circumstances, 1942 to 2012: a chronology, Parliament of Australia.* Retrieved from http://www.aph.gov.au/About_Parliament/Parliamentary_Departments/Parliamentary_Library/pubs/BN/2012–2013/SSPaymentsUnemployment.

Farrow, K., Hurley, S., & Sturrock, R. (2015, December). *Grand Alibis: How declining public sector capability affects services for the disadvantaged.* Discussion paper from Centre for Policy Development. Retrieved from https://cpd.org.au/wp-content/uploads/2015/12/Grand-Alibis-Final.pdf

Foucault, M. (1985). *The history of sexuality, vol. 2: The use of pleasure.* (trans. by Robert Hurley). Pantheon Books.

Foucault, M. (2008). *The birth of biopolitics: Lectures at the Collège de France, 1978–1979.* (trans. by Graham Burchell). Palgrave Macmillan.

Fowkes, L. (2011, March). Rethinking Australia's Employment Services. Sydney: Whitlam Institute. Retrieved from https://www.whitlam.org/data/assets/pdf_file/0004/181183/Rethinking_Australias_ Employment_Services.pdf

Frings-Sen, M. H. W., Hoving, J. L., Audhoe, S. S., & Sluiter, J. K. (2010). Vocational interventions for unemployed: Effects on work participation and mental distress. A systematic review. *Journal of Occupational Rehabilitation, 20*(1), 1–13. https://pubmed.ncbi.nlm.nih.gov/20039106/

Ganley, R. (2002). The psychological impact of joblessness. *Australian Social Policy 2002–03.* Australian Government. Retrieved from http://www.forschungsnetzwerk.at/downloadpub/Australia_2002_2003_socialPolicy_2004.pdf#page=183

Gass, J. (1988). Towards the active society, *OECD Observer, 152*, 4–8.

Graham, L. (2011). The product of text and 'other' statements: Discourse analysis and the critical use of Foucault. *Educational Philosophy and Theory, 43*(6), 663–674.

Handler, J. F. (2003). Social citizenship and workfare in the US and Western Europe: From status to contract. *Journal of European Social Policy, 13*(3), 229–243.

Harris, P. (2001). From relief to mutual obligation: Welfare rationalities and unemployment in 20th century Australia. *Journal of Sociology, 37*(1), 5–26. 10.1177/144078301128756175

Henriques-Gomes, L. (2020), Robodebt court documents show government was warned 76 times debts were not legally enforceable, *The Guardian*, https://www.theguardian.com/australia-news/2020/sep/19/robodebt-court-documents-show-government-was-warned-76-times-debts-were-not-legally-enforceable

Immervoll, H., & Scarpetta, S. (2012). Activation and employment support policies in OECD countries. An overview of current approaches. *IZA J Labor* Policy, *1*, 9.

Jahoda, M. (1982). *Employment and unemployment: A social-psychological analysis.* Cambridge University Press.

Jobs Australia. (2012, November 23). *APESAA final report: Jobs Australia feedback on final report and government response.* Retrieved from https://www.ja.com.au/sites/default/files/jobs_australia_response_to_the_apesaa_final_report.pdf

Marston, G., Zhang, J., Peterie, M., Ramia, G., Patulny, R., & Cooke, E. (2019). To move or not to move: Mobility decision-making in the context of welfare conditionality and paid employment. *Mobilities, 14*(5), 5.

McClure, P. (2000). *Participation support for a more equitable society: Final report of the Reference Group on Welfare Reform.* Department of Family and Community Services.

McDonald, C., & Marston, G. (2005). Workfare as welfare: Governing unemployment in the advanced liberal state. *Critical Social Policy, 25*(3), 374–401. 10.1177/0261018305054077

McGann, M., Nguyen, P., & Considine, M. (2020). Welfare conditionality and blaming the unemployed. *Administration & Society, 52*(3), 466–494.

Mead, L. (1986). *Beyond Entitlement*. Free Press.

Mead, L. (1997). *The new paternalism: Supervisory approaches to poverty*. Brookings Institution Press.

Mendes, P., Roche, S., Marston, G., Peterie, M., Staines, Z., & Humpage, L. (2020). 'The Social Harms Outweigh the Benefits: A Study of Compulsory Income Management in Greater Shepparton and Playford', *Australian Social Work*, Epub ahead of print 8 October 2020. 10.1080/0312407X.2020.1820536

Mestan, K. (2014). Paternalism in Australian welfare policy. *The Australian Journal of Social Issues, 49*(1), 3–22. 10.1002/j.1839-4655.2014.tb00297.x

Mills, C., & Klein, E. (2021) Affective technologies of welfare deterrence in Australia and the United Kingdom. *Economy and Society, 50*(3), 397–422. 10.1080/03085147.2021.1875692

Moreira, A., & Lødemel, I. (2014). Chapter 11. Governing activation in the 21st century. In Lødemel I. and Moreira A. (Eds.), *Activation or Workfare?: Governance and Neo-liberal Convergence*. Oxford University Press.

Morrison, S., & Porter, C. (2016). *The Coalition's Plan for Better Management of the Social Welfare System*, viewed 22 February 2021, https://cdn.theconversation.com/static_files/files/1050/turn1.pdf?1590734108

Neville, A. (2013). The curse of accountability: Assessing the relationships in the delivery of employment services. *The Economic and Labour Relations Review, 24*(1), 64–79. 10.1177/1035304612474214

O'Donnell, A. (2019). *Inventing unemployment: Regulating joblessness in twentieth-century*. Bloomsbury.

O'Halloran, D., Farnworth, L., & Thomocaos, N. (2020). 'Australian unemployed workers' experiences of being parked and creamed by employment providers. Australian Journal of Social Issues. Epub ahead of print 4 September 2020. 10.1002/ajs4.131

OECD. (2012). 30 YEARS OF THE OECD EMPLOYMENT OUTLOOK Its historical beginnings, evolution and future direction as a major policy engine. https://www.oecd.org/els/emp/30%20YEARS%20%20OECD%20EMO%20final.pdf

OECD. (2012). *Activating jobseekers: How Australia does it* (1. Aufl. ed.). OECD.

Organisation for Economic Cooperation & Development (OECD). (1990). OECD Economic Outlook, 1990. Australia, Hart. https://www.oecd.org/employment/emp/4153026.pdf

Parliament of Australia. (2014). *Explanatory memorandum, Social Security Legislation Amendment (Stronger penalties for serious failures) Bill 2014*. Retrieved from https://www.aph.gov.au/Parliamentary_Business/Bills_Legislation/Bills_Search_Results/Result?bId=r5275

Parsell, C., Clarke, A., & Perales, F. (2021). The role of charity and the cultivated ethical citizen. *Poverty by design: Social Policy and Society*, Advance online publication https://doi.org/10.1017/S1474746421000312

Peterie, M., Ramia, G., Marston, G., & Patulny, R. (2019). Emotional compliance and emotion as resistance: Shame and anger among the long-term unemployed. *Work, Employment and Society, 33*(5), 794–811.

Pinto, M. (2019). Exploring activation: A cross-country analysis of active labour market policies in Europe. *Social Science Research, 81*, 91–105.

Productivity Commission. (2002, June 2). Independent review of Job Network: Inquiry report. Report No. 21. Retrieved from http://www.pc.gov.au/inquiries/completed/job-network/report/jobnetwork.pdf

Rose, N. (2000). Community, citizenship, and the third way. *American Behavioral Scientist*, *43*(9), 1395–411. /0.1177/00027640021955955

Sage, D. (2013). Activation, health and well-being; neglected dimensions? *International Journal of Sociology and Social Policy*, *33*(1/2), 4–20.

Sage, D. (2019). Unemployment, wellbeing and the power of the work ethic: Implications for social policy. *Critical Social Policy*, *39*(2), 205–228.

Senate. (2009). DEEWR tender process to award Employment Services contracts. Report from the Senate. Retrieved from http://www.aph.gov.au/~/media/wopapub/senate/committee/eet_ctte/completed_inquiries/2008_10/employment_services/report/report_pdf.ashx.

Senate. (2019, February). Jobactive: *Failing those it was intended to serve*. Canberra: Education and Employment Reference Committee. Retrieved from https://www.aph.gov.au/Parliamentary_Business/Committees/Senate/Education_and_Employment/JobActive2018/Report

Services Australia. (2021). Mutual Obligations. *Services Australia*. Retrieved from https://www. servicesaustralia.gov.au/individuals/topics/mutual-obligation-requirements/

Staines, Z., Marston, G., Bielefeld, S., Peterie, M., & Mendes, P. (2020). 'Governing Poverty: Compulsory Income Management and Crime in Australia'. *Critical Criminology* Advanced online publication. 10.1007/s10612-020-09532-2

Thomas, M. (2014). *Social Security Legislation amendment (stronger penalties for serious failures) Bill 2014* [bills digest]. Commonwealth of Australia.

Thomas, M. (2018). *Jobseeker compliance and workforce participation*. Retrieved from https://www.aph.gov.au/About_Parliament/Parliamentary_Departments/Parliamentary_Library/pubs/rp/BudgetReview201718/JobSeeker

Van Berkel, R., & Van der Aa, P. (2012). Activation work: Policy programme administration or professional service provision? *Journal of Social Policy*, *41*(3), 493–510. 10.1017/S0047279412000062

White, S. (2004). What's wrong with workfare? *Journal of Applied Psychology*, *21*(3), 271–284.

Wong, V., & Au-Yeong, T. (2018). Expediting youth's entry into employment whilst overlooking precariousness: Flex-employability and disciplinary activation in Hong Kong. *Social Policy & Administration*, *53*(5), 793–809.

Wright, S., & Patrick, R. (2019). Welfare conditionality in lived experience: Aggregating qualitative longitudinal research. *Social Policy and Society*, *18*(4), 597–613. 10.1017/S1474746419000204

Yeend, P. (2004). *Mutual obligations/work for the dole: E brief.* Social Policy Unit, Australian Government. Retrieved from https://www.aph.gov.au/About_Parliament/Parliamentary_Departments/Parliamentary_Library/Publications_Archive/archive/dole?print=1

5

AFFECTIVE GOVERNING AND THE PSY-COMPLEX

Introduction

In the previous chapter, I analysed *jobactive* policy as one of many 'nodes' assembled to 'resolve' the problem of unemployment. *Jobactive* continues the focus on 'work first' and ensuring job seekers 'participate' in the labour market through practices of activation. *Jobactive* represents an increased focus on penalising the unemployed. The *jobactive* deed provides the 'rules of the game' for providers to organise their spaces, develop 'innovative' SDPs and use discretion to attune these practices to individual 'needs'. In this chapter, I focus on case management strategies as enacted in one employment services provider ('Active Job') to explore governing practices under *jobactive*.

Employment consultants or *jobactive* workers ('workers') are infused with various types of authority to enact policy and encourage changes in job seekers' behaviour. Workers are called upon to employ affective governing strategies to activate (through motivation, empathy, enthusiasm) or to 'undo affect' (through the diffusion of anger, management of conflict, etc.) (Penz et al., 2017). In other words, workers engage in self-governing practices (building rapport, maintaining eye contact and other embodied strategies) to ensure their interactions with 'jobseekers' (clients) produce 'soft skills' (motivation, dispositions, attitudes). Across different employment services in different welfare regimes, these practices often imply detailed interpersonal interaction and evoke psy-complexified notions about the self, thoughts, behaviours and emotions, including motivation, disgust, shame and deterrence (Glisner et al., 2018; Gřundělová, 2020; Pultz, 2018; Yang, 2015). Indeed, some of the critiques of ES in Australia also psychologise the treatment of unemployment by assuming that ES workers should be qualified in psy-related disciplines assuming that unemployment is a problem that could and should be addressed through psy knowledges (Jobs Australia, 2012; Senate, 2019).

DOI: 10.4324/9781003112518-5

These affective and psy practices are institutionalised insofar as they are dis/allowed through contractual and organisational procedures and priorities.

Much front-line research on ES tend to focus on interactions between workers and clients. Research has looked at how the unemployed are encouraged to see themselves as passionate about careers while also ashamed for receiving welfare, emphasising the psychological components of embodied emotions (Pultz, 2018). Research has also looked at the potential for emotional labour to soften punitive activation (Nguyen & Velayutham, 2018) or how workers can make emotional and embodied decisions to help certain migrant clients (Volckmar-Eeg & Vassenden, 2021). However, research looking at emotions and/or affect in governing the unemployed can reinscribe psychologised notions of emotion by not critiquing counselling practices or the assumptions underpinning the identified affect. To address this gap, I follow McAvoy (2015) and Wetherell (2012) by positioning 'emotions' within discursive practices and by exploring how emotions are involved in the production of subjectivities. Using Poststructural Interview Analysis (PIA) (see Bonham & Bacchi, 2017) I take the interview text as a point of departure to explore 'what was said' instead of 'who said what', and thereby locate discursive practices and ongoing formations of objects, subjects and spaces. I use interviews and observations to identify problematisations, showing how unemployment and the unemployed are constituted through the practices of Active Job (AJ).

My interest is to highlight how participants from AJ problematised unemployment as a procedural issue that didn't require 'heart-to-heart' or personal interactions between workers and clients. I outline how the service delivery program (SDP or 'GROUP') mirrored some of the discourses that underpin *jobactive* policy. Namely, the SDP assumed a 'passive' client who needed to be 'activated' to ensure they 'participated' in the labour market. I discuss how workers problematise GROUP by 'emotionalising' the spaces of ES, and situating themselves and clients as potential subjects. Here, at the conjunctions of 'work-first', 'activation' and psychologised discourses, the unemployed subject becomes (re)psychologised through 'emotion'. Unemployed subjects are discursively positioned as 'sad', 'bad' and 'mad'. The ideal unemployed subject was expected to remain enthusiastic despite continual setbacks. As I will discuss, these practices relied on psy-infused notions about empathy, and therapeutic encounters. This analysis also considers the potential for transformation from the multifarious and diffuse discourses and power relations that overlap or collide in these spaces. I discuss how psy-infused 'emotions' became 'heart technologies' that informed, activated and sustained the problem of the unemployed.

Problematising individual case management

SDPs are activation programs that encompass many types of activities. They include mandatory job searching, along with other activities such as learning interview techniques and self-development activities that a provider may use as part of their case management toolbox. These procedures also act like a map for workers to guide their daily work activities. In the literature, there is discussion about ES workers using interviews and personal interactions with clients as a tool of pastoral power, namely to elicit personal information from the client that is suggestive of a confession (Boland, 2021; Pultz, 2018). Such confessional interactions form part of the governing strategies workers use to 'motivate' the unemployed to look for work and self-govern to improve job readiness. The confession was part of an array of affective governing strategies where workers would wield emotions such as 'empathy' (doing affect) or stop emotion, for example, defusing anger (undo affect) as a means of working with, and activating, the unemployed (Peterie et al., 2019; Penz et al., 2017; Glisner et al., 2018). The SDP as enacted under *jobactive* limited the possibility for confessional interactions, which in turn curtailed how unemployment could be positioned as an 'emotional experience'.

According to the participants, the SDP solved the problem of the previous contract and SDP which was based in individual case management. The problem was that clients were supposedly doing nothing while they waited for individual appointments. Additionally, individual appointments had no 'active components', again leaving clients sitting 'passively' while the worker completed the administrative side of the appointment, such as updating Job Plans or checking compliance to other activities. Participants described appointments as administrative exercises, "tick and flick" (Jay,[1] WS1[2]) that didn't require much engagement from clients. In short, the SDP rendered the clients' 'passive'. To rectify this 'problem' the SDP rearranged the office spaces of AJ, transforming them into open-plan 'activating spaces'. There were fewer sitting tables, and instead, there were standing desks (although high chairs were provided). Combining the spaces for 'waiting' with spaces for 'training' limited the possibility for clients to sit and wait for an appointment; thereby the spatial organisation disallowed the (assumed) 'passive' subject. An interviewee explained the model thus:

> I guess my understanding is that (.)[3] [workers] are up there (2) with the clients [job seekers] then it is giving them the um (1) the right kind of motivation to be doing it themselves just to help them out when they need help (.) really it is up to them to do their own job searching to find their own job (.) but we have got to have certain activities which will help promote (.) will help them become job-ready or get to that point where we can send them out to interviews confident that they are ready (mmhmm) so but it's it's (1) putting it back on them to do the actual work (.) so when someone says that they can't do resumes 'well here is the computer (.) here is the tools here is the template so what you can (.) start it (.) if you need assistance we will do what we can'.
>
> *(Shay, EC,[4] NS2, first interview)*

I focus on 'what is said' by participants to analyse what is 'sayable' or acceptable (Bonham & Bacchi, 2017, p. 117). In chapter Four, I demonstrated that the discourses that underpin welfare policy over time, namely activation and participation, target an imaginary despairing subject. Activation, implicitly acknowledges that unemployment 'causes' despair and people lose motivation (as per psychological literature, see Chapter Three for discussion). The overlap between the policy objectives and the everyday enactment is detectable in these 'activities' that should keep people engaged in looking for work and attached to the labour market. The GROUP model as explained by Shay evokes these same discourses insofar as ES should keep clients 'motivated' to "do the actual work" of jobseeking. The aim to 'activate' the unemployed through group case management relied on the self-responsibilised subject to lead their own job search or 'do the work', while workers embody an administrative subject. The assumed 'active' client is mobilised through space by limiting the possibility to be 'passively waiting'; self-led activities were supposed to keep clients 'activated' for the entire appointment.

Providing set tasks for the clients was part of the set of practices that made unemployment a technical problem. By rendering unemployment technical, something that could be alleviated through simple tasks (such as how to write a cover letter), the GROUP constituted the unemployed as lacking practical or technical skills. The subject is also presumed to be *homo economicus*, a rational, self-interested, decision-making, subject who could or should respond favourably to self-led activities and see the benefit of self-improvement to increase the chances of being quickly (re)employed. Correspondingly, the new SDP altered the 'how' and the 'what' of governing, by slightly adjusting how workers could and should engage with clients.

I was able to sit in on the morning team meetings at NS2. At one such meeting early in the research, the employment consultants discussed the difficulty clients were having adjusting to the new SDP, particularly around the limited interpersonal elements. Workers portrayed clients as wanting to divulge personal issues during appointments. One worker, tongue-in-cheek, remarked that some clients "just want to talk about their dead cat" (Fieldnotes, NS2, 30 October 2015). The problem here was clients were only allowed to discuss their active engagement towards finding a job. That is, there were 'rules' being laid down that only certain things were 'sayable' in these spaces, and with this, only certain emotions can be expressed and discussed. The reference to a 'dead cat' signals a hierarchy of emotions, with certain objects being too trivial to deserve empathy from employment consultants. These 'rules' extended to the role of employment consultants who do not deal with 'dead cats' or the emotions, feelings, detail or complexity accompanying loss; "we are not psychologists" was the general agreement at the meeting. These 'heart-to-heart' conversations, either trivial or substantial, were presented as irrelevant to the spaces of AJ:

> Yeah yeah no need to ask them how they are (.) (yea) bullshit (.) please (.) you know (.) you've got to start their conversation with 'g'day how're you going' or or 'how's your day going' or 'what've you been doing? What've you been up to?'
>
> *(Sal, LEC, SS1)*

To avoid distraction from the task at hand, workers would have to 'undo affect' and minimise 'heart-to-heart' interactions. The removal of personal conversations established 'affective rules' (Penz et al., 2017) around permissible language and communication devices in these spaces, as Sal explained, "no need to ask them how they are". Such a thing is 'sayable' within work-first discourses where unemployment is constructed and performed as a technical problem. These new affective rules established the basis for governing from a distance both morally and ethically.

With unemployment positioned as a technical problem, the worker's role was also technical and administrative. These problems were evoked when workers' problematised their daily work and explicated a mismatch between their expectations of clients and cleints' expectations of the workers/ES. These lines were also drawn in emotional terms between activating clients and "getting bogged down and becoming their counsellor" (Jay, EC, WS1). In the following extract Saroo and I are talking about the Job Plan and the unchangeable 'goal' section, which stated clients had to be looking for work and the impact this had on worker-client interactions:

ROSE: do you think though with the ability to craft a goal firstly it made it more individual to the person so they could have their you know, short-term goal medium-term goal long-term goal but it also gave you a little bit of scope to (3) address goals that maybe aren't (2) so-ah-work focused in the short term but in the long term they would be so if you were working with a guy who is I'm going to go to extremes here and say=

SAROO: =a doctor=

ROSE: well I was actually going to say a drug addict right who is going to rehab *S airy laugh* the first goal is to get off drugs right *S laughs* and then you move down that way

SAROO: look um the *jobactive* is all about jobs (ah huh) so we talk about jobs (.) if there is a health area like I mention before that is something to discuss with Centrelink

ROSE: so you don't have those conversations? Because we used to have those conversations?=

SAROO: =we used to have those conversations=

ROSE: we used to have um=

SAROO: =and we used to hold onto those clients for years (ah huh) we have notation for 8 years seeing psych for 11 years seeing a GP for 12 years it doesn't help it cost the individual their life to continue in that trend and we encouraged that for so many years (Saroo, LEC, second interview, NS1).

The interview exchange suggests that the clients should not 'confess' themselves, their situation or any mitigating circumstances that suggest nuanced, textured or complicated lives and corresponding job search trajectories. Two different sets of discourses are evident in the excerpt. Firstly, clients are pathologised through health and psychologised discourses that create a 'needy' and 'addicited' client.

However, the ongoing practices of the interview shift, and the problem is no longer that conversations are needed to 'help', but that these conversations are actually the problem. Consequently, the subject positions available for workers and clients are also re-formed. In contrast to the affective governing that is needed to 'help' those who are 'addicted'; the 'semi-neo-bureaucratic' worker emotionlessly undoes affect to stop these 'irrelevant' conversations that render clients 'dependent'. The second set of discourses, activation and 'work-first', underpin how employment spaces are rendered emotional-neutral in the interivew by emphasising the bureaucratic purpose of AJ, "*jobactive* is all about jobs, so we talk about jobs". These practices are also positioned as moral concerns because conversations make people dependent on welfare payments and cause harm, "cost the individual their life". Here 'care and concern' intersect with 'work-first' discourses to produce employment as beneficial to a person's 'wellbeing'. In other research, the affective labour involved in activating clients is positioned as either enacting feminised care work, or affect-neutral masculine bureaucratic work (Glinser et al., 2018). The subject positions portrayed in the above extract, however, can be interpreted as subsuming 'care' into masculine non-affective labour. This type of work is produced as more effective at activating and 'helping' clients, subsequently, the feminised aspects of 'heart-to-heart conversations' are devalued.

Interpreting these ongoing formations of practices (and related subject positions) creates spaces to examine the politics that shape case management and influence wider research practices. PIA highlights how there are multiple readings of a text and all readings have political implications (Bonham & Bacchi, 2017). Psy discourses can be read as legitimising authoritarian governance or they could be seen as potentially disruptive. From a mainstream psychological position, removing the scope for understanding individual distress, and referring on, might be seen as problematic. As a consequence, researchers may recommend workers are trained in 'mental health', the 'effects' of unemployment, and psychological programs of reformation (workers' lack qualifications in 'psy' related disciplines has have been noted as a 'problem', see Chapter Four). Conversely, the analytical focus could higlight how confession practices are enabled through psy-complexified strategies (Hook, 2004b) such as using emotional performances of 'empathy', probing and positioning the self as fixed, stable and understandable through excavation of the soul. The removal of these confessional/emotional strategies opens the possibility for also dismissing psy-complexified discursive practices in AJ.

By making compliance contingent on participating in psychological interventions, even mundane practices like 'confessing the soul', the social and economic inequalities of unemployment are erased; unemployment is re-made as a matter of individual pathology (Friedli & Stern, 2015). This British research suggests that psy knowledges provide a sheen of legitimacy and authority to authoritarian governance practices. From a critical psychological perspective, the removal of 'heart' conversations in AJ could arguably be an opening for potential transformation by providing other nodes in the apparatus to allow for new directions. The removal of 'confessional' practices presented possibilities for understanding unemployment, and its 'effects', in non-psychological ways.

In contrast, most of the interviewees took issue with the new SDP and how this rearranged their work duties and the possibility to use affective governing. These problematisations reform subjects so they "become psychological" by "simultaneously troubling and [making] intelligible" clients and governing practices "in terms that are infused by psychology" such as a "psychological taxonomy" of "abilities, personality, attitudes" (Rose, 1996, p. 60) and 'emotions'. The subject positions taken up by workers are fluid and in-formation since they are always walking a "fine line". The opportunity to govern by 'doing affect' is diminished in the GROUP setting. Fortier (2011) positied governing through affect involved sculpting opportunities for "meaningful interactions" (p. 22) for shaping people as subjects. The GROUP model made no allowances for emotional subjects outside of the 'assumed' 'appropriate emotions' (i.e. motivated and 'job ready'). Removing the conversation to discuss more 'emotional' aspects of clients' lives discursively de-constituted the emotional subject. However, the de-constitution of the emotional subject is not fully achieved. In the ongoing processes of self-formation, interviewees (and the interviewer) (re)emotionalised (and (re) psychologised) clients and themselves. Below I discuss how the interviews evoked psychologising discourses and constituted the unemployed as problematic emotional subjects: 'sad', 'bad', and 'mad'.

(Re)psy-complexifying the unemployed

The de-constitution of an 'emotional' unemployed subject was problematised by most workers I interviewed (cf. Saroo). Indeed, workers discussed their workspaces as *emotional* spaces, within which both clients and workers were positioned as emotional subjects. These emotional discursive practices reinserted psy-complexified practices into the discussion about how to activate the unemployed. By complicating the processes of activation, the workers (and the researcher) re-subjectified the unemployed as 'sad', 'bad' or 'mad'.

Sad subjects

problem.Psy-complexified practices in AJ emotionalised subjects in ways that affirmed the authority and purpose of *jobactive*. These practices evoked worker's expertise in 'knowing' the unemployed through a psy-lens that saw them as enacting problematic emotions and inner lives. Simultaneously, these psy-complexified practices demonstrated the limitations of positioning unemployment as a technical

KAREN: 'cause it is really about their self-esteem and building them up to feel good again (hmm) 'cause we all know that they have been unemployed for a period of time and I call them a millionaire with no money because they have as much time as a millionaire but you know though to get get back into their restriction (.) that discipline again and resilience it takes it takes you have got to let those guards down to get back in and to conform I suppose to get back into the working life again and I feel it is people like myself to when I when you have been out of work for 12 months that is a long time to go to developing even bad habits in regards to

ROSE: Bad habits?

KAREN: I believe I feel bad habits could be we have an unemployment cycle that we were training in the past contract it's called the 'unemployment cycle'

ROSE: I haven't heard of that, yep

KAREN: yea and it starts of quite you (.) the periods in between the emotional self (hmm) you know start off on long snapshots but that it starts to becomes quite quickly on the waves of you are not feeling good about yourself (.) over a three to six months that cycle of how you are feeling about yourself changes (hmm) because you have been not working for 6 months, so it does affect (yep) your self-esteem (Karen, EC, WS1).

Workers discussed how 'heart' conversations helped to excavate the personal information they 'needed' to activate clients. Clients were seen as living complicated emotional lives that 'caused', was an 'effect of' or kept clients unemployed. In other words, the 'heart' conversations were needed because unemployment was not regarded as a 'technical' problem. In the excerpt above emotions are seen as 'causing' "bad habits", resulting in "not feeling good" through an "unemployment cycle". The psychological gaze, or psychologisation, refers to the influence of psychological discourses to frame problems and solutions, by turning onto oneself (or in this case 'others'). Reflection about 'behaviours' 'moods', 'attitudes' and such forth is understood within vaguely defined psychological terms (De Vos, 2012). The client "become[s] psychological" (Rose, 1996, p.60) since their emotions (low self-esteem), tied to how they think and act ("bad habits"), and marks the person out as 'being unemployed' by fitting the "unemployment cycle". Unemployment is constituted not just through what it is possible to 'say' about the unemployed but also how the unemployed 'feel'.

'Becoming psychological' through the psychological gaze is also about ensuring people constantly 'feel' the need to work upon and improve the self in specific ways (Burman, 2017). The gaze here is focused on identifying and then working on the 'sad' subjectivities of unemployed, helping to reform them into "feeling good" about themselves and boosting 'self-esteem'. 'Self-esteem' is not neutral but deeply embedded within political practices that link the personal to appropriate social behaviours, social stability and organisation (Cruikshank, 1993). Ensuring that clients have improved self-esteem improves the ability of the worker to withstand the detrimental impact of being unemployed, but also creates more resilient surplus labour for a changing labour market. Here, psychologising discourses run parallel to 'work-first' discourses and activation discourses that underpin *jobactive* policy as laid out in the previous chapter.

Making bad and mad subjects

Clients were also discussed in the interviews as being emotional subjects insofar as they were not displaying a range of emotions and associated behaviours deemed 'acceptable'. In other words, clients were positioned as being emotional in the 'wrong way', usually non-compliant, thus marking them out as 'bad' and 'mad':

> He sat down over in the corner over there and he was uh I thought he was up because almost virtually talking to himself but it looked like he was talking to himself he was down like this but he had the earphones in and he was on the phone to uh I don't know to who but just the aggression in his voice (mm) I had an office full of people there was even a parent with a small child in here (mm-hm) and he was all 'F this and F that and blah blah' and I said "mate you're going to have to settle down" and he just looked at me and he's just gone "I'll do f' what I like f' when I want to" right? "don't you dare tell me what to do (.)" So I said "Mate I'm not telling you what to do I'm just saying settle down or get out (hmm) alright? That's all I am saying that's uh not open for discussion" (mm) he says "are you threatening me?" and I said "no just ju-(1) finish your phone call outside all right (ah huh) and then come back in" (.) he's got picking it all up "you can all go and get" them that's fine see you later (.) so you're right did he attend? No he did not (.) I marked him as not attended.
>
> *(Sal, LEC, SS1)*

Sal maintained the client did not 'attend' the appointment because he did not 'participate' in an acceptable manner. According to policy, clients are considered to have 'attended' an appointment if they "arrived on time at the correct location, behaved appropriately, and participated for the duration of the appointment" (Department of Employment, 2017b, p. 8). Thus, deciding what is 'acceptable' behaviour in the spaces of ES relies on discursive practices that establish what one can say, 'within the true'. The client is here discursively positioned as being outside of the grid of acceptability within the spaces of AJ through this inappropriate display of emotions. It is through the 'gaze' made possible by the open 'activating spaces' of AJ that this client is marked out as a problem.

Having constituted the client as aggressive and acting in a 'weird' unintelligible way – talking (supposedly) to himself and cursing loudly, Sal evoked an authoritative subject position, maintaining the social order of the space by directing the client to "settle down". In turn, the client is attached to the subject position of 'bad', because he is 'mad'. The non-compliant client is 'angry', 'aggressive' and 'irrational'. These subject positions are formed through psychologised discursive practices that make 'sayable' and 'thinkable' 'common sense' notions of appropriate behaviours (not talking to oneself, using emotional regulation to contain anger in a public space, especially when engaging with an authority). Moreover, the psy-complex sustained the emotionalising of spaces through Sal's description of his affective governing.

With the client produced as irrational and aggressive, the worker had to 'undo' this emotion by using affect to assert control and remove the 'problematic' client. Undoing anger was a consistent problem raised by workers:

> Well it is if they are job ready they are fine but they're doing their own job search like that girl you know what I mean? You know they're doing the work and they are fine and if they are not job ready they're just sitting here angry (.) whereas if it was a one on one you are taking that away.
>
> *(Jay, EC, WS1)*

This 'anger' could be defused through individual case management assuming the psy-complexified notion that through working with someone at a personal level emotion can be contained and, potentially, address "all these issues". Anger is positioned as a problem to be 'solved' rather than a legitimate response to injustice (Peterie et al., 2019). Worker's capacity for affective governing was reduced by a model that disallowed engaging ethically and emotionally with the clients. However, across the interviews, the 'practice' of 'heart conversations' was not a straightforward solution to activating an emotional unemployed subject.

> Yea probably not so inclined to be over sympathetic towards people's situations not that I don't have any but you like it's not our work it's fix it yourself you know (.) because we do see people like counsellors people treat us like counsellors (.) I had a man the other day he has broken up with his wife and he had a form to fill out and he filled out everything on the form with things like 'equal rights for men' you know all that anger was just coming out and it was coming right at you so you know you have got to learn to (2) put up a barrier.
>
> *(Shay, EC, NS2, first interview)*

These 'heart' practices are produced in Shay's interview as 'doing', and 'undoing' affect through self-governing. Shay had to "put up a barrier" in response to the 'mad' (read: angry) client. Unlike other workers who discussed 'heart' conversations as necessary to elicit to personal information for activation, Shay depicted clients as the ones who create these 'counselling' or confessional situations. Affect management also pathologised clients' desires for empathy/understanding undermining their 'context'. Psychologised discourses are evoked here in order for these 'counselling' interactions to be truthful, and for the 'not so over sympathetic', and 'angry' subjects to be understood as such. Moreover, the 'irrationality' of the angry client that displays too much emotion in the wrong setting requires established norms about socially acceptable and situated displays of emotions. In this account, Shay again reiterated the discourses around excluding emotional and 'counselling' type work from the ES space. What is different about Shay's account is that the emotions of the unemployed subject cannot be contained and so workers needed to "learn to put up a barrier". In the transcript, the clients' emotions activated the worker to disengage emotionally.

Intertwined with governing the unemployed is how workers are governed and self-govern. So far, I have discussed the governing of the governed to minimise affective governing and make activation more 'efficient' and unemotional. The governing of governing actors is partly achieved through official forms and organisational practices that reshaped the SDP, and therefore instructed workers on how they 'should' activate clients. I have also discussed how reforming case management limits how workers could deploy conversations as a technology, restricting affective governing strategies. Furthermore, workers drew upon psychologised notions of the self as an emotional subject to self-govern through affect.

In the interviews, psy-complexified notions of the emotional subject also activated workers to reshape governing practices for clients. In the excerpt below Ray problematised the GROUP model on the grounds of 'lack of participation' and, therefore, lack of activation. This is a notable moment of differentiation (Bonham & Bacchi, 2017, p. 116) because it flagged how the GROUP SDP produced the same problem as individual case management, namely, clients were not being activated.

RAY: same sort of reaction to the group activities (.) I think (1) the first session we did was like a video session so we got them down to watch a video for 20 minutes and that did not work because there was no participation really um and =

ROSE: = is that the video where there are a set of slides and someone talking over the top of it?

RAY: yep, and you can barely hear the talking? Yep that one *laughs* Yep so um that was basically my first three weeks here and I was looking at it going "that video just does not work", and you could see people going (1) you would see (1) that the red flags were popping up in the room and you could see people becoming very (.) resistant the body language the crossed arms and stuff they were not engaging (hmm) (.) so what I found was that doing something that involved them actually hands-on doing something has actually eliminated some of that (ok) because they are actually seeing that they're doing something they are not just here to get their names marked off and then to go away for three weeks (Ray, LEC, NS2).

In Ray's transcript, the training videos are produced as de-activating technologies, failing to engage clients in the content because the video is poorly made. Accordingly, the GROUP model is understood as reducing appropriate client participation. Instead, participation proceeds through embodied resistance. 'Participation' is privileged in activation discursive practices because the focus is on ensuring clients are "doing something" while they are at their appointments. Here 'Ray' is produced as a 'perceptive' worker and 'ideal activation worker' subject who notices the 'red flags' by observing "that video just does not work". He uses initiative to create a GROUP that (aimed to) ensure clients "are not just here to get their names marked off". Again, slients are assumed to be passive unemployed subjects who need to be motivated to look for work and engage in the labour market.

Psychological discourses are used to produce the worker who is able to identify "red flags". For example, by interpreting the body language of the client as resistant. This 'type' of client is not ideal, and so the 'perceptive worker' reformulates governing practices towards the end goal of ensuring clients are "doing something". The perceptive worker supposedly uncovers the resistant clients' psychology and sees the 'solution' as reshaping clients' inner processes or perceptions. The issue here about ensuring clients are participating demonstrates how questions around how best to govern the unemployed depoliticise the problem and its solutions. That is, the interviewee/er challenge the quality of the video rather than the content or purpose of the video. The problematisations as operationalised through individual case management, the organisation of offices spaces, heart-to-heart conversations and the GROUP model, all appear to 'fail' in the quest to ensure clients participate in predetermined ways. Psy-complexified 'truths' allow workers to 'know' themselves and the clients whose behaviour is targeted for change around lack of participation. But activation failures still occur. Despite these lapses, ES continues to be positioned as a legitimate space for the activation of clients.

Psy and heart technologies as potential transformation

As I discussed in Chapter One, the affective governing literature on ES passes over the role of psy-complexified knowledges in its critique. Consequently, I went beyond affective governing by looking at the different ways in which, what I call 'technologies of heart', were mobilised. I suggest that emotions or 'heart', as they are produced through the interviews, was more than a rationalisation for governing practices. D'Aoust's (2013) uses the concept of emotion as a technology in and of itself. For D'Aoust, affective governmentality is limited to how emotions form part of the rationalisation of the 'conduct of conduct'. She argued that affective governmentality misses how emotions affect governmentality. That is, in her work she discusses how emotion, "shapes conduct through expectation of its 'true' manifestation by the 'feeling subject'" and "'connects citizenship and intimacy'" (p. 264). Similarly, I suggest psy-infused 'emotions' became 'technologies of heart' that informed, activated and sustained the problem of the unemployed and associated governing practices.

Technologies are practical rationalities that aim for a certain goal but they also constitute subjects and organise life on contingent principles. As Rose (1999) describes, technologies require connection between an ensemble of power-knowledge, skills, devices, judgements, capacities and skills. D'Aoust (2013) too recommends tracing the materiality of technologies as they move back and forth between the self and the collective via practices, artefacts, language and words, and spaces. In my research, 'technologies of heart' were deployed to 'activate' clients through 'conversations' (practices), motivational inscriptions (artefacts), reframing clients as 'candidates' on a journey (language), and through the 'activating' spaces or more 'hands-on training activities'. Heart technologies activated clients to stay motivated, but also activated workers to reshape their governing strategies. The heart technologies constituted through the interviews also laid a terrain of knowledge and skills around how to read and work upon the clients or what workers *should* be doing but can't because of GROUP.

There is also then the question of heart technologies as power-knowledge that could open up potential for transformation or rethinking governing the unemployment. PIA encourages the researcher to look for avenues of potential transformation analysing text for moments of contradiction, ambiguity or contestation of dominant discourses (Bonham & Bacchi, 2017). However, these moments are marked by potentiality and partiality. For example, Ray differentiates the ability of certain clients to 'get and keep' a job and through this adds nuance and complexity to challenges one of the unemploymed stereotypes:

> yea it does I think I guess (1) people are not really, well you hear people saying "oh well it's not hard to get a job" and (2) look there are people who come through the door who literally could go out and get a job tomorrow if they you know really put their mind to it (.) but there are many people who come through the door who need much assistance to get a job.

Clients are divided into two groups: those who could easily get work but choose to be unemployed, and those who need help. There are resonances with the deserving and undeserving binaries associated with the Poor Laws. These accounts of job search held potential to challenge dominant discourses about deservingness and moral citizenship. As Ray continued,

> You are not just dealing with that fact, you need to get a job, it is everything else (.) and you know, having people sitting down in front of you and telling you 'oh I have my plan to kill myself tonight' and how you deal with that (.) you have got to have that emotional resilience to get through that. Looking at the picture of oh I will just go and get a job it is not that easy especially when you are dealing with all these extra factors out (.) there how do you combat that?

For many of the interviewees the loss of 'heart conversations' meant they had lost a 'tool' for governing clients with people with complex issues, often framed in terms of 'mental health'. There is potential for 'psy' to disrupt activation discourses by adding complexity such as by engaging with the emotions of the unemployed. The unemployed subject is produced as being *more than* passive but also depressed and suicidal. Alongside the emotional client is the worker who, in the text, has to manage the complex and emotional problem of activating clients "dealing with all these extra factors" (Ray, LEC, NS2). The worker had to self-govern (becoming resilient) in order to manage 'irrationality' (drink driving). Consequently, the task of motivating clients to 'do the work' of finding a job is fraught with nuances that are outside the worker's expertise, "how do you combat that?" The ongoing formation of objects and subjects in the interviews meant unemployment became *more than* a technical issue (so getting a job first is no longer the obvious solution) and the unemployed became *more than* just unwilling to find work.

The subversive potential of psychologising unemployment is small. One issue is that the 'mental health' of clients is presented as the explanation for why it is 'harder' for certain cohorts to find a job. There are two main concerns that I would like to raise here. Firstly, 'mental health' is a regime of truth that presents a certain way of understanding distress. Mental health is legitimated through medicalising discourses, with potentially pathologising effects (Holmqvist, 2009). Secondly, psychologising unemployment in this way ignores how 'unemployment' and 'mental health' are entangled with economic, social and political practices (Boland & Griffin, 2015), meaning that distress is unevenlly distributed through soceity. Although there is potential to challenge the 'work-first' discourses of *jobactive,* the client, pathologised through the psy-complex, is still unable to find and keep a job because of something wrong with them as an individual. As Bonham and Bacchi (2017) suggested, we should check our research to see if, as researchers, we are challenging or (re)producing pervasive thinking. Here is an example of how the research (re)produced pervasive thinking about the unemployed as not only deficit but dangerous ("was he drunk?"). Psy still contributes to the marginalisation and pathologisation of unemployment and does little, if anything, to politicise the 'problem' of unemployment. In this way, heart technologies activated, informed and sustained activation practices and blamed the unemployed.

Concluding comments

Activation is constantly being reconfigured in a bid to govern the employed. Where once individualised case management was upheld as good practice, this would later be seen as not having the desired effects, producing deactivation instead. A key part of this problem was the way workers could and should do their governing work. Engaging clients in 'heart-to-heart' conversations are seen as irrelevant and de-activating. In this way, my research follows previous literature by highlighting how organisational priorities (see Marston, 2013) and policy context (see Jordan, 2018) remake what 'governing' the workers can do in their daily work. Using an ethnographic imagination and situating *jobactive* as an apparatus has moved past programmatic renditions of *jobactive* implementation (see Chapter Three). *Jobactive* policy sets the conditions and activates providers to deliver services to prioritise job placements within activation and work-first discourses. It is unsurprising then that the SDP developed by AJ turned the management of the unemployed into something technical, thereby making governing an administrative exercise and obscuring the politics of activation. In the worker's accounts, they described how their daily job duties were focused on 'undoing affects' of the 'sad', 'bad' and 'mad' clients.

Affective governing practices put emotions to work to create specific desirable outcomes (Penz et al., 2017). In AJ the objective is to get the unemployed to 'feel' motivated, enthusiastic, determined and optimistic about the future. To make sure clients are 'job ready'. For many participants, the main problem in the interviews was the loss of the 'heart-to-heart' conversations, their mechanisms to diffuse tension and 'activate' or motivate the clients. Emotions identified in the transcripts made certain unemployed subjects 'visible' and assessable according to psychologised knowledges. These grids of intelligibility shaped practices of the self, the potential self and legitimised particular ways of talking about and 'experiencing' emotions. What was 'within the true' 'emotionally' provided the rationale for establishing deficiencies in the case management of clients. These problematisations collectively contribute to producing the experience of unemployment as 'psychologised' by "simultaneously troubling and [making] intelligible" (Rose, 1996, p. 60) clients and governing practices through a psy-complexified understanding of emotions.

Technologies of heart situate clients as *not* 'job ready', making them 'recognisable' instead as 'sad', 'bad' or 'mad'. These 'feeling subjects' are identified by watching how clients 'act' and use the office space ('displaying resistant body language'), how they 'speak' (swearing at self or workers), use artefacts (writing 'rights for men' on paper) and assumptions about how they 'should' be feeling because they are unemployed (low 'self-esteem'). These practices, which include artefacts, space and language, are 'knowable' as 'truthful' through psychologised discursive practices. But these heart technologies do more than inform; they also activate and sustain dominant problematisations of unemployment.

In the interviews, clients are produced as deficit subjects, needing help to find work and become 'emotionally' job ready. This included being encouraged to develop confidence and 'good habits', being punished for misbehaving in a public space and being 'pulled back' from engaging in dangerous behaviour. The emotional displays of clients are 'signs' that knowing workers can identify and address. The technologies of the heart are made reciprocal, where the 'feeling subject' (client) activates another 'feeling subject' (worker) to conduct themselves and the clients differently. For example, in Shay's interview, she takes up a feeling subject position where she is activated to utilise technologies of the self to guard against angry clients and in turn, alters her ability to do affective governing (show empathy).

In Ray's interview, the client's emotions activated workers to reshape GROUP activities. Moreover, in Ray's interview, heart technologies highlighted how rendering unemployment technical was idealised but incomplete. Here, unemployment was produced as emotional but in a way that escaped the function of ES and the worker's expertise. Unemployment as a problem of 'heart' exceeds the rationalisation of governing practices. However, in all of the examples, 'activation' is never fully unpacked or subverted. Instead, heart technologies help to sustain the objectification of the unemployed *as* the problem of unemployment. The potential for utilising psychological knowledges to challenge the practices of ES was detectable in these interviews but ultimately fell short.

To sum up, while research suggests that we need to attend to the problematisations on the ground, this chapter shows that we can also add that researching the governing of unemployment requires attuning to how 'emotions' function in these spaces. 'Affective governing' is nuanced by psy-infused 'emotions' that informed, activated and sustained the problem of the unemployed. These concerns correlate with and overlap with discursive practices in other places. Indeed, looking at *jobactive* as an apparatus, we can trace how the relations of practices between different sites converge on the bodies of the unemployed if they fail to embody neoliberalism. They come to be placed on the periphery of moral citizenship.

Notes

1 Participant names have been replaced with pseudonyms.
2 The four research sites were West Site 1 (WS1), South Site 1 (SS1), North Site 1 (NS1), North Site 2 (NS2).
3 Interviews were transcribed verbatim. As with any other research practice, transcription is not straightforward or politically neutral process. I have tried to limit interpreting sound by editing words into sentences or statements, although I concede there is always some interpretation and the transcripts are hardly 'objective' but open to multiple readings. The codes are: (.) signals a pause, (2) signals a pause of two seconds, = run-on sentences, (ok) provides the minimal responses from the other person and ** signals extra-material aspects such as laughter.
4 EC – employment consultant or worker; LEC is Lead employment consultant.

References

Boland, T. (2021). Avowing unemployment: Confessional jobseeker interviews and professional CVs. *Foucault Studies, 30*, 31–53. https://rauli.cbs.dk/index.php/foucault-studies/article/view/6256

Boland, T., & Griffin, R. (2015). Introduction and general remarks. In T. Boland & R. Griffin (Eds.), *The Sociology of Unemployment*. Manchester University Press.

Bonham, J., & Bacchi, C. (2017). Cycling 'subjects' in *ongoing-formation*: The politics of interviews and interview analysis. *Journal of Sociology, 53*(3), 687–703. 10.1177/1440783317715805

Burman, E. (2017). From subjectification to subjectivity in education policy research relationships. In J. Lester, C. Lochmiller, & R. Gabriel (Eds.), *Discursive Perspectives on Education Policy and Implementation*. Palgrave Macmillan.

Cruikshank, B. (1993). Revolutions within: Self-government and self-esteem. *Economy and Society, 22*(3), 327–344. 10.1080/03085149300000022

D'Aoust, A. (2013). In the name of love: Marriage migration, governmentality and technologies of love. *International Political Sociology*, 7, 258–274. 10.1111/ips.12022

De Vos, J. (2012). *Psychologisation in times of globalisation: Concepts for critical psychology, disciplinary boundaries rethought*. Routledge.

Department of Employment. (2017b, June). Guideline: Managing and monitoring job seeker appointments. Version 2.0 Accessed 17 December from https://docs.employment.gov.au/system/files/doc/other/managing_and_monitoring_job_seeker_appointments_2.pdf

Fortier, A. M. (2010). Proximity by design? Affective citizenship and the management of unease. *Citizenship Studies, 14*(1), 17-30. 10.1080/13621020903466258

Friedli, L., & Stern, R. (2015). Positive affect as coercive strategy: Conditionality, activation and the role of psychology in UK government welfare programmes. *Medical Humanities, 41*, 40–47.

Glinser, B., Sauer, B. Gaitsch, M., Penz, O., & Hofbauer, J. (2018). Doing gender in public services: Affective labour of employment agents. *Gender, Work & Organization, 25*(3), 1–17.

Gřundělová, B. (2020). Client experience of street-level activation practices: Implementation of discourage policy in the Czech Republic. *Critical Social Policy*. 10.1177/0261018320980583

Hook, D. (2004). Governmentality and technologies of subjectivity. In D. Hook (Ed.), *Introduction to Critical Psychology*. UCT Press.

Holmqvist, M. (2009). Medicalization of unemployment: Individualizing social issues as personal problems in the Swedish welfare state. *Work, Employment and Society, 23*(3), 405–421. https://doi.org/10.1177/0950017009337063

Jobs Australia. (2012, November 23). *APESAA final report: Jobs Australia feedback on final report and government response*. Retrieved from https://www.ja.com.au/sites/default/files/jobs_australia_response_to_the_apesaa_final_report.pdf

Jordan, J. D. (2018). Evidence from the 'frontline'? An ethnographic problematisation of welfare to work administrator opinions. *Work, Employment & Society*. Advanced online production 10.1177/0950017017741238

Marston, G. (2013). On 'activation workers' perceptions': A reply to Dunn. *Journal of Social Policy, 42*(4), 819–827. 10.1017/S0047279413000482

McAvoy, J. (2015). From ideology to feeling: Discourse, emotion and an analytic synthesis. *Qualitative Research in Psychology, 12*(1), 22–33.

Nguyen, T., & Velayutham, S. (2018). Street-level discretion, emotional labour and welfare frontline staff at the Australian employment service providers. *Australian Journal of Social Issues, 53*(2), 158–172. 10.1002/ajs4.35

Penz, O., Sauer, B., Gaitcsh, M., Hofbauer, J., & Glinser, B. (2017). Post-bureaucratic encounters: Affective labour in public employment services. *Critical Social Policy, 37*(4), 540–560. 10.1177/0261018316681286

Peterie, M., Ramia, G., Marston, G., & Patulny, R. (2019). Emotional compliance and emotion as resistance: Shame and anger among the long-term unemployed. *Work, Employment and Society, 33*(5), 794–811. 10.1177/0950017019845775

Pultz, S. (2018). Shame and passion: The affective governing of young unemployed people. *Theory & Psychology*. Advanced online publication retrieved from http://journals.sagepub.com/doi/pdf/10.1177/0959354318759608.

Rose, N. (1996). *Inventing ourselves: Psychology, power and personhood*. Cambridge University Press.

Rose, N. (1999). *Governing the soul: The shaping of the private* self (2nd edition). Taylor & Frances/Routledge.

Senate. (2019, February). Jobactive: *Failing those it was intended to serve*. Education and Employment Reference Committee.

Volckmar-Eeg, M. G., & Vassenden, A. (2021). Emotional creaming: Street-level bureaucrats' prioritisation of migrant clients 'likely to succeed' in labour market integration. *International Journal of Social Welfare*. https://onlinelibrary.wiley.com/doi/full/10.1111/ijsw.12510

Wetherell, M. (2012). *Affect and emotion: A new social science understanding*. SAGE.

Yang, J. (2015). *Unknotting the heart: Unemployment and therapeutic governance in China*. Cornell University Press.

6

UNPACKING INTERVIEWS, UNPACKING UNEMPLOYMENT

Introduction

The second chapter highlighted that research practices should be critically coherent since the method and methodology are interlinked with tackling how psy knowledges govern the unemployed. Research is productive insofar as the objects, such as the 'experience(s) of unemployment', "are formed by the very practices through which they are known" (Parker, 2005, p. 3). I draw on ontological politics to attend to how research intervenes in the world (Mol, 1999). The driving question for this chapter is, what subjects and objects are produced by the methods used? This chapter engages with 'knowledge' in a non-epistemological frame to 'suspend' interviews and reflexively unpack the assumptions and implications.

This chapter engages with reflexivity from a critical perspective, focusing on the constituting elements of research. Taking such a reflexive position involves examining the theoretical, ideological, epistemic assumptions that influence how research practices unfold (Burman, 2017; Pillow, 2015; Subramani, 2019). I explored these concerns by using reflexivity as an opportunity to examine how the research problematised the object under study – thus examining how the research *produced* the object as a certain kind of problem (Bacchi, 2012). In this way, I also included the seventh process of Poststructural Interview Analysis (PIA, Bonham & Bacchi, 2017), the politics of distribution, to consider how interviewing practices challenged or reinscribed pervasive ways of thinking (as described in Chapter Five). Thus, reflexivity does not just look at how practices could have been done differently, changed or omitted but also opens other lines of inquiry to study the power-knowledge nexus. I take the above reflexive focus on methodology to examine my research practices for epistemic, political and ethical implications.

DOI: 10.4324/9781003112518-6

Epistemic implications of truth-telling in a critical research study

In this front section, I explore the assumptions that underpin how research practices are enacted and how these cohere (or not) with a Foucauldian-inspired frame-of-reference. I touched on this issue in previous chapters. I noted the methodological and analytical gaps left when governmentality approaches are merged with traditional fieldwork practices (see Chapters Two and Three). I bridged these gaps with the 'apparatus' and PIA (Bonham & Bacchi, 2017). However, I think there is still work to be done to think through what it means to 'do' Foucauldian-inspired research methods. In the more easily recognisable 'formal' analysis process, the data needs to be positioned appropriately (from the way the interview was done and justified) to make it amenable to a particular type of analysis (Braun & Clarke, 2021; Frith & Gleeson, 2011). These processes are often done before or after the research has finished, and less attention is paid to the *doing* of research to ensure that we do not inadvertently (re)produce assumptions that we are rejecting, dismissing or problematising. Indeed, it was this very issue that Larner (2008) warned could be an unintended effect from merging governmentality approaches with traditional social science methods in that objects or subjects under scrutiny become 'self-evident'. The task should be to *trouble* rather than *reinscribe* unemployment and the related distress.

As I noted in Chapter Two, I wanted my research to be critical. I drew on one of the insights from critical psychological research: the importance of being explicit about our research's assumptions and philosophical underpinnings because we know what these assumptions *do* in mainstream critical psychology (see also Chapter Three). In short, the issue here is that while I provided a way to justify how the method could be strung together and analysed, I could not satisfactorily justify the enactment of methods in the same way. Playing between these different sets of 'rules' exposed the research to different criteria, that of 'good' governmentality research and that of 'good' qualitative fieldwork. Thus, at times, the research practices are caught in the in-between, producing methodological tension. Casting a reflexivity lens onto my research, I use this space to lay bare these unsolved difficulties and implications. I will focus on the 'interview' since my research relies heavily on this research practice.

The challenge of traditional methods: The interview

A difficulty in finding a Foucauldian-like way of doing fieldwork is that Foucault did not do fieldwork. Admittedly, he did do plenty of interviews, and these interviews constitute a large and influential part of his work, supplementing (although sometimes contradicting) his published books and lectures. Nevertheless, these interviews are not used to understand Foucault as a person, his inner thoughts and so forth. Interviews can create all sorts of problems for poststructuralist researchers. Interviews can be used to explore discourse but they can also resubjectify beucase interivews interactions are produced through discourse. My focus here is on unpacking how research pracitces are enacted and what assumptions such enactments bring into the research assemblage.

Bonham and Bacchi (2017) stated that interviews "entail a highly policed set of procedures" (p. 7) that produce 'truth', 'objects' and 'subjects'. They encourage researchers to think about how the questions asked (re)produce or challenge 'pervasive thinking'. However, like the governmentality researchers using an 'ethnographic imagination', Bonham and Bacchi did not elaborate on *how* enacting research practices (such as building rapport or transcription) have political implications. The focus was on analysis *after* the interview rather than *how* to do a Foucauldian or critical interview. I am interested in how a research interviewer would interview Foucault in a 'Foucauldian-inspired poststructuralist' manner. And in doing so, also provide a way to justify claims made from these research practices that are consistent and (meta) theoretically coherent.

Toulmin (2003) argued that there is a difference between making a claim, the ground of agreement for a claim ('evidence' or 'data') and warranting (the theorisation of why and how the evidence are connected to the claim). These processes are linked to how a practice, for example, interviewing, is enacted. Research methods are epistemically informed practices formed by a set of research techniques making methods distinguishable. So, we should be able to recognise differences between different methods such as Photovoice (Wang & Burris, 1997) or Grounded Theory (Glaser & Strauss, 1967). While there are claims to broad generic definitions of interviewing (usually as a conversation that generates data to be analysed, see Gubrium & Holstein, 2016) and criteria to establish 'good' interviewing (Roulston, 2010), 'interviewing' materialises differently depending on method and methodology.

Following then, it should be possible to compare and contrast interviewing in different methods. Indeed, Brinkmann and Kvale (2018) stated that interviewing, as a technique, is a 'craft' and has its own 'peculiarities' that can be identified, packaged and taught. In turn, attached to these practices will be assumptions about the purpose of the interview, the interviewer/ee, appropriate behaviours and interactions, and what constitutes 'data'. For example, Brinkmann (2013) presented two broad categories of interviewing that require different 'styles' (borrowing from Wengraf, 2001). Brinkmann describes interviewing as a "research instrument" (p. 37) that assumes the interview reflects the interviewees' reality outside of the interview and captures 'experience' in a post-positivist sense. Such interviewing invokes a 'receptive' style where the interviewee is considered the 'expert' and provided open questions to elaborate on the topic.

In contrast, interviewing as a "social practice" (Brinkmann, p. 39) assumes interviewing is a social interaction where knowledge is co-produced and uses an 'assertive' interviewing style. This style is more akin to interrogation where the interviewer is trying to provoke, illuminate and to some degree control the responses of the interviewee. All of these practices will need to be coherent with the method and methodology of the research chosen.

Different approaches to interviews, with their respective interviewing 'style', highlight the taken-for-granted assumptions that underpin interviewing practices regardless of whether researchers make this assumption explicit in their methodology. These assumptions are tied into dominant discourses about the role of research and how to access certain types of 'knowledge' about 'individual' or 'collective experiences'. Brinkmann (2013) noted, the 'receptive style' is often considered to be "self-evidently right" (p. 31) and thus forms the core style that gets reproduced uncritically in qualitative studies. Therefore, without being explicit about our research processes, we can (re)produce practices, such as a 'receptive style' in Foucauldian-inspired research projects. Does allowing the interviewer to speak 'freely' about their experiences as an 'expert', fit with an 'ethnographic imagination' in a study that is heavily influenced by Foucauldian-inspired poststructuralism? It may do, but it is not 'self-evidently right'. Researchers need to do the knowledge work to make these links explicit to ensure the claims made are warrantable. As practices of 'truthing', these practices are thus acceptable ways of doing and producing 'evidence' that can be warranted as a claim. What counts as knowledge and what objects/subjects are produced (the connection between power and knowledge) is intrinsically connected to the concerns about fieldwork and knowledge work done in an academic assemblage.

Making sure all these moving parts cohere (meta)theoretically requires work: generating the research question, the way the interview is positioned (what type of data is needed, what is the role of the interviewer and participant, etc) if the interview is done well in order to produce appropriate data that can then be analysed using appropriate analytical procedures. The data are subsequently warranted and used as 'evidence' to defend claims made by the researcher, reinserting the claims into a conversation with the appropriate literature. Interviewing as a technique thus fits into the collection of practices and devices, interwoven with theory, to achieve research aims. How knowledgementing is done, regarding generating research questions, producing a literature review, explaining methodological assumptions, methods and the appropriate techniques therein all come together and cohere. Regardless of whether the reader agrees with them, the claims made are nevertheless taken seriously as 'knowledge'. A theoretical link needs to be explicated between different stages of the knowledgementing process to ensure practices are all consistent with what the research espouses to be about.

Warranting claims in an 'ethnographic imagination'

The unresolved issue in my research is that it is unclear how to justify interviews as they are enacted from a Foucauldian-inspired poststructuralist perspective without reinscribing contradictory assumptions about 'knowledge', the subject, 'experience' (as self-evident instead of the constituted) and objects. A part of this trouble goes back to the same issue I raised with governmentality researchers who utilised an 'ethnographic imagination'. The ethnographic imagination does not follow dogmatic methodological prescriptions of classic anthropological renditions of ethnography but still relies on the general premise of what makes ethnography different as a research practice. Brady (2016) stated she used Forsey's (2010) term 'ethnographic imagination' to describe these new research practices that rely partly on the accounts of situated actors. These 'accounts' of situated actors come from research interviews. While researchers claim they are moving beyond method to a 'sensitivity' they still engage in social science research practices, mostly demonstrating 'quality'. By doing the work to demonstrate 'good quality research', we must make transparent our research practices and draw on language (and thereby regimes of truth) that make methods intelligible (making our claims justifiable). So, researchers who use an 'ethnographic imagination' still use the traditional social research method of interviewing and justify this method according to mainstream (and not necessarily critical) methodological criteria and do not often include how their research practices both study subjectification and are also subjectifying or reproducing the pre-discursive 'I' through research practices (see Chapter Two). A lack of examination of the practice of research, especially interviewing 'individual thinkers', could (re)produce the psy-complex.

The 'ethnographic imagination' borrows from Forsey's (2010) idea that research can be interview-led and still be 'ethnographic' insofar as researchers think ethnographically. By this, Forsey meant interviews can be used like participant observation to access the details of the cultural world of the cohort under investigation. In participant observation, interviewing as a technique is about gathering details from people's accounts about their lives and world. Interviews are often positioned as exploratory, with interview questions developing 'organically' in situ (Gobo, 2008). The importance of being in the situation to gather as much detail about a person's life and social world is steeped in the assumption that ethnography enables the researcher to access information that would be otherwise difficult to obtain. For example, Britzman (2000) used Foucauldian concepts and ethnography because her topic "required my presence in the world of student teachers" (p. 10) in order to research how student teachers learn to teach. Even though Collier (2013) stated that ethnography is not necessary, he argued it does allow the researcher to come into contact with problems they may not otherwise see, hear or learn. The interview in an 'ethnographic imagination' still needs to be tied to method and methodology as a technique because it is an epistemically informed practice. The enactment relies on certain assumptions about how knowledge is produced, the role of the researcher and the purpose of research. When we start pulling at the assumptions of interviews in ethnography, the 'criticalness' of our research starts to come undone. I made three attempts to forgo these issues as I was *enacting* the interviews during fieldwork, as separate from *analysing* the interviews with PIA once the interviews were completed. I will discuss two attempts here.

An interview by any other name

Brinkmann and Kvale (2018) provide a guide to researchers on how to design an interview study. They describe what is expected of a 'good' interview study and, for my purposes, show how the taken-for-granted assumptions create methodological tension within my critical frame-of-reference. The authors suggest that researchers clearly state the purpose of the interviews, what is being investigated, and how the intended knowledge is to be obtained. There are additional questions for a critical study like mine to also cohere with the four axes I mentioned in Chapter Two. How do we present and justify the interview or observations or other forms of fieldwork in a way that rejects the pre-discursive/humanist individual, refusing the psy-complex; presents knowledge as a verb and interlinked with power relations and refusing to make epistemological claims? What was the purpose of the interview? What were the knowledge-producing conversations assuming? Who was the imagined interviewee, and what was the role of the researcher? What style of interview techniques should they use, and how could these be justified?

The issue is 'how' interviews can be practised as a technique to allow these governing practices to be discernible from the data without contradicting the critical frame-of-reference. I made two attempts to try and reconfigure the interviews during my research to try and resolve different issues connected to doing Foucauldian-inspired research. Firstly, the interviews were positioned as 'guided conversations' rather than 'interviews'. Following the work of Laing (2008), 'problematising' interviews were also imagined to challenge the taken-for-granted assumptions in situ. Any attempt to 'reimagine' the interviews made very little difference. In short, the completed interviews are not distinguishable from any other ethnography that sees interviews as a research instrument to produce 'data'. In the discussion below, I expand on how I attempted to reimagine 'how' to do a Foucauldian-inspired interview from a pre-fieldwork perspective.

'Recorded conversations'

In the first instance, knowing that the interview was not a 'perfect fit' with the Foucauldian-inspired study, I thought ethnographic type interviews or 'recorded conversations' would be a way through the mire. Such 'conversations' are ethnographic and emergent since they are led by interaction in the situation and could gather the details of the research situation: interactions, rituals, behaviours, artefacts (or discursive and non-discursive practices) (Gobo, 2008). Interviews positioned 'merely' as conversations might be helpful to rethink the power dynamics of an interview (Fontana & Frey, 2005). Indeed, such purposeful conversations may contribute to dynamic sense-making and encourage the respondent to take the lead in the flow of the discussion (McGrath et al., 2018). Such research practices may challenge the traditional interview (that follows a schedule) if researchers dominate the situation. However, such renditions of a 'conversational interview' are not 'critical' in the sense of 'critique'. In a Foucauldian-inspired purview, power is capillary and multifaceted so that both the interviewer and the interviewee are produced in various ways through power relations. While the interviewer might have the authority to 'control' the conversation, the interviewee is often infused with the 'authority' of their own experiences and feelings (Bonham & Bacchi, 2017).

Using these conversational/ethnographic interviews employs a 'receptive' style (Wengraf, 2001) that is open-ended, allowing the interviewer to direct the conversation with the interviewer prompting for more detail. 'Good' interviewing for ethnography should gather 'rich data' (Fetterman, 2019) and in my research would include what is happening in the situation, changes in the workplace service delivery, and explore the worker's experiences, thoughts and feelings about these changes. Trying to ascertain more detail about practices, artefacts and the everyday life experiences of the workers also positions the interview as an 'instrument' (Brinkmann, 2013) to be used in conjunction with a receptive style (Wengraf, 2001).

Interview data can be used as evidence for an analytical claim once it is demonstrated that it is relevant and was produced by an appropriate method for the analysis. For example, presenting a text segment from an interview transcript might be a worker describing a situation where a client failed to attend an appointment. Presenting the interview transcript as 'data' of something that has 'really happened', of thoughts and feelings of workers that are deemed to be 'going on', and 'representative' of the practices 'on the ground' in employment services requires a realist methodology within an ethnographic method. The 'data' produced through interviews is assumed here to be "an empirical reality in which those words exist as brute data independent of the interpretive desires of the data 'collector'" (St Pierre & Jackson, 2014, p. 716). I left this idea behind them since not only was it not a 'perfect fit', but it raised other problems.

Problematising interviews

Interviews, as discursive practices, can produce certain types of subjects, potentially shutting down possibilities for being otherwise. Interviewing can be individualising by establishing the research participant as an 'individual', and often, this means a pre-discursive subject (Bonham & Bacchi, 2017). The trouble here is that interviews reproduce a 'psychological' subject. The interview (in an interview society) encourages people to 'confess' their inner selves, experiences and meaning-making processes. These confessional practices are often psy-complexified (Parker, 2005). Interviewing is incoherent in a Foucauldian inspired because Foucault (2002) himself was trying to avoid the 'psychological', and it tends to lead the research to focus on the 'individual'; instead of the practices that make that 'individuality' possible. Can we interview a person without individualising or psychologising them, the issue, ourselves? The main concern I had with the final and most promising 'experiment' was 'problematising interviews'. Following the work of Laing (2008), these interviews were trying to challenge the dominant discourses of employment services by bringing the taken-for-granted assumptions to the fore. The task was to politicise the conversations, moving them away from the description of opinions and practices to the co-troubling of taken-for-granted assumptions of practices in these employment services spaces. In this way, dominant discourses about unemploy(ed) ment in this sector should be exposed, unpacked and unsettled. Problematising interviews would be less 'excavating' people's experiences or reframing issues and more like a discourse analysis in situ (Parker, 2005). The most exciting aspect of these reimagined interviews was, for me, the potential to use the interview to be subversive (not just uncover or find subversion).

However, just like with the 'conversations', there was an unscalable barrier to enact interviews that cohered (meta)theoretically with my frame-of-reference. Take this interview excerpt as an example. At this point, the 'participant' (Saroo) is explaining the new Service Delivery Plan[1] (SDP) as a 'hard mattress' and the researcher (Rose) presents an alternative understanding of the 'problem' of the 'depressed' client ('job seeker'):

SAROO: People were used to that (.) they were used to the fact that "I am depressed I have a problem I'll go to Salvation [Army] and seek counselling for the next three years (.) it's like a soft bed if you are used to a soft bed you can only sleep on a soft bed and if you are used to sleeping on a hard mattress you can sleep on a hard mattress it's very much like that (.) so *jobactive* is very much like a firm if you have got bad back get yourself a hard mattress (ah huh) just fix it (ah huh) can you excuse me for a moment *speaks to client in the hallway**turns back to Rose* yep *starts typing*

ROSE: because that is interesting though, because the psychological literature on unemployment (yes) they talk it in terms of the effects of unemployment has on people and it kind of the longer you are unemployed the kind of worse than it is for you (.) and so do you think you should not not have those feeling those heart to heart conversations with that sort of information in mind? (Saroo, LEC, NS1)

Problematising interviews might not present opportunities to enact 'critique'. Instead, problematising interviews may trouble dominant discourses by drawing on another dominant discourse that may be just as troubling. The position that the 'depressed' unemployed need a 'hard mattress' (as opposed to counselling) is 'countered' and problematised by psy-complexifying unemployment as something that gets 'worse' without interpersonal 'intervention'. Such discourses intersected repeatedly in the research interviews (and was raised in the previous chapter). The problem of the unemployed is 'spoken' 'truthfully' within activation and work-first discourses. These practices are re-problematised with references to unemployment causing mental health issues. As noted in Chapter Five, psychologised discourses push against the dominant discourses in Employment Services, and are partial and problematic. Rather than 'discourses crossing swords' (Tanggaard, 2007), the interviewing technique constituted the unemployed as unmotivated, dependent or depressed.

I do not want to suggest that the interview was done poorly or that the 'problematising' element could be improved. I want to draw attention to how the topic under discussion is constituted in the 'event' of the interview, the research and the spaces where the interview occurred. The interview constructs the 'condition of possibility' for research participants. So, stepping outside the dominant discourses (activation; work first; unemployed have poor subjective wellbeing) is harder to enact in situ because discourses are entrenched in these ES spaces (see Chapter Four). In a research study that is trying to challenge the psy-complex, the difficulty in trying to refuse to understand the unemployed as passive, lazy, cheating or as 'depressed' or 'anxious' (at least not in the dominant psychologised constructions) meant I often challenged the notion of the 'lazy jobseeker' with the 'depressed client'. By 'problematising' the unemployed as 'depressed' (psy pathology), the interview (re)produced unemployment as a psychological issue.

The two interview types exposed several issues with enacting interviews that all, in turn, present challenges for warranting research claims. How do you cohere a research approach that (meta)theoretically challenges the individualising (especially assuming a pre-discursive subject), psychologising, generating evidence or accessing the 'real' (instead of researching discourses) with interviewing practices that either relies on these assumptions to make sense as a research technique or has these effects when enacted? It is also important because our research practices have political implications (Mol, 1999). I discuss the political implications of how research is enacted in the following section by looking closely at the 'insider/outsider' issue in ethnography as it was relevant in my study. This conversation is related to how to warrant research claims because it raises the problem of how to 'select' participants and how to engage in research interviews as an 'insider' or an 'outsider'.

Making participants visible as an 'insider'

In this section, I extend this discussion about the subjectification of interview practices by attending to the types of subject positions made available through enacting interviews in an 'ethnographic imagination'. The 'insider/outsider' issue in ethnography provides an avenue for demonstrating the political implications of interviews.

Participating as 'employment consultants': Making up participants

Before I discuss the 'insider/outsider' problem, I will discuss 'who' the 'insider' is produced to be. The participants were to be employment consultants of an employment service provider. Identifying the workers as interviewees subjectifies participants as certain types of subjects. Firstly, as Foley (2012) notes, "to conduct particular kinds of research ... researchers must imagine a certain type of respondent" (p. 305). I assumed that workers could and would discuss their daily work practices. Secondly, and more importantly, I marked them out as 'employment consultants' and nothing else by selecting the workers as participants. Fadyl and Nicholls (2013) suggested an interview is a discursive event wherein power, both productive and capillary, individualises subjects by identifying them as individual subjects. Thus, designing and conducting interviews "imposes a law of truth on him [sic] which he must recognise and which others have to recognise in him [sic]" (Foucault, 2003, p. 130). Fadyl and Nicholls argued that using sampling to locate participants makes them 'visible', marking them out as a particular subject. Workers in employment services do governing work and are governed as workers (as is discussed in Chapter Six about the changes to the SDP). There is minimal scope in the interview event to discuss oneself and one's work outside of the research parameters, even more so since the interviews were done in the workspace. Participants could only 'take up' the position of 'employment consultant'.

Limiting the potential for 'being otherwise' may have limited the critical potential of the research. Looking back at research practices with a reflexive lens highlights how the enactment of research may not cohere (meta)theoretically but also raises other questions. In establishing the research purpose with employment consultants (and following procedures such as providing information sheets and gaining informed written or verbal consent), I would sometimes identify myself as 'one of you' because I previously worked in employment services. Therefore, I presented myself as both an 'outsider' (interviewer) and an insider ([former] employment consultant). Building rapport and establishing some credibility to encourage people to participate or answer questions in this way is occasionally considered an important researcher skill (Creswell, 2013). I would often begin interviews this way to help create a comfortable atmosphere. Considering that the interviews mostly occurred in the openly planned workspace, this idea of creating a 'comfortable atmosphere' depoliticises the interview location, ignoring the power relations and how they are "produced, reproduced, and challenged continuously during the interview process" (Herzog, 2012, p. 216). These relations extend to the interview location and what it is 'safe' to say about work practices in an open plan office where colleagues, superiors and clients are potentially within hearing distance.[2] Where the interviews occurred then curtailed what subject positions were available through the interview event. The institutional and discursive practices that produced the space and how bodies moved through it were a part of what was 'sayable' in the interview 'event'. In this way, the knowledge produced through interviews is partial and situated but also political.

The spaces of employment services are political and contested. Beyond what it is 'safe' to say about work practices, as I discussed in Chapter Five, the design of the office space established what practices were allowable for clients *and* workers. The interview event is wedged into these practices during the research, forming part of the discursive practices, such as socio-spatial/temporal arrangements, that produce subjectivities. The provider offices were open-planned but also local and bounded. Since space is "fundamental in any exercise of power" (Foucault, 1982,

p. 361), we can look at how practices that establish, maintain or transgress boundaries contribute to what workers can do *as* workers and then what can be said in interviews. I'll draw on some field notes from NS2 to explicate this point:

> I arrived by bus at NS2 at about 0820. The bus stop is just around the corner from the front of the office. As the bus rode over the last hill and the office came into view, I could see about ten or so people hanging out the front of the office. This struck me as strange. I was early since I wanted to try and get into the office prior to the door officially 'opening' to see if I could be part of the 'heads up' – the part of the day where the workers organise their day and communicate with other sites about problems, possibilities for future practice and other organisational concerns. The front doors were locked. I waited with everyone else. Though it was early in the morning, the summer sun was already starting to become unbearable. The doors should have been opened at 0830, and it was 0840, and the doors were still locked. I walked around the front where some of the jobseekers were waiting. It's 0845 and one guy was knocking on the door, trying to peer through - its futile since the glass is reflective. I stand next to him to see if there are any messages on the door alerting us here waiting about possible delay; there is none and I say as much. Without looking at me he remarks, "we should dock their pay since they are late". The doors open at 0850. No explanation was given to the group. Shay pulls me aside later to tell me they [workers] had to lock the doors because they had some kind of staff training on and no one could be spared to monitor the floor had they opened on time.
>
> *(Fieldnotes, NS2, 9 December 2015)*

Once those front doors of the office (described above) were opened, we crossed a boundary into a space where workers have some authority to enact policy and procedures. The suggestion that workers should have their pay 'docked' for opening the doors late references a change made to the *Social Security Act* where clients can temporarily lose part of their pay for not coming to an appointment (see Chapter Four). Turning this idea on its head, the client's remarks signify a disparity in who gets to define, organise and monitor the use of time in these spaces. Shay pulling me aside to provide more details about why the workers did not open the office on time could be presented as an example of the 'insider' performance 'working'. Getting those extra details adds nuance to an analysis by illuminating how organisation practices, such as inadequate planning, resourcing and under-staffing, impact the workers' ability to enact policy or use discretion to resist or rework these practices. The governing of the unemployed *and* the governing of the workers are entangled processes in these provider offices.

This does not suggest that the distribution of 'being governed' is shared equally (Rasmussen, 2013). There are differences in who is taken seriously and who is placed at the centre of reformation practices according to the provider's organi-sational hierarchy, between jobseekers and workers, and between the provider and other organisational bodies. While interviewing practices 'make up' possible subject positions, the 'insider/outside' component of ethnography-as-usual can subvert the usual 'stories' of workplace practices or reinscribe them. I continue with the line of inquiry in the section below.

'Working the hyphen'

It is tempting here to claim that having a prior understanding of the research spaces from a (former) 'insider' perspective was beneficial because I have 'experience' doing this work. Alternatively, to claim 'insider' status may immediately assume there is an opposite 'outsider' status, and it may be implied that this outsider status may hold more validity since as an 'insider' the researcher may be blind or unwilling to document certain practices (Creswell, 2013). Maintaining such a dichotomy is uncomfortable in poststructuralist research since subjectivities are seen as fluid, fragmented, incomplete, contradictory and open to transformation.

Critical research tends to move beyond focusing on 'insider' or 'outside' categories as absolute and focus on the nuances and partially of such standpoint or performativity (Kerr & Sturm, 2019). Cairns (2013) asserted the 'insider/outsider' status is interesting regarding what counts as 'insider', 'outsider', what knowledge is linked to these divisions, and how such practices impact participants. Here I focus on "working the hyphen" (Fine, 1994), trying to blur the distinction between the self-other by writing 'myself' into the research reflexively as an interviewer-employment consultant. I argue 'insider status' helped to co-construct certain stories about the governing work of ES and the possibility of worker subjectivities therein.

For example, the below transcript excerpt could be positioned as demonstrating the rapport-building and story-sharing practices of an interview. Both interviewer (Rose) and interviewee (Shay) exchange their shared experiences of being overworked in an understaffed workplace. Shay is discussing how the worker in her office have rescheduled their work day in order to finish their work tasks because "in the past we're so understaffed that you just don't get the resulting done" and then I soon interrupt her:

ROSE: yeah sorry I'm having those little flashbacks of when I used to work in this industry *laughter* I remember then (.) when I first started I was they put me on like a trainer for the groups sessions (.) and I had to do that and I had to write the job search because I was doing (.) oh (.) one on ones (.) two different kinds of training sessions (.) and the job search so I was doing two people's jobs because they only put on one casual (oh my gosh) as you do (1) and it was like only for a very short period of time and I was like (yeah) whatever I need the work (.) and I remember getting there at eight to try and get everything set up in time like I'd have to go through and get all the training manuals ready (.) make sure that you sent out the text reminders (.) and all of those sorts of things (2) and I remember that I didn't eat lunch (.)

and I lost so much weight (.) I didn't eat much *laughter* trying to get through (.) and it was things it was the resulting that took forever (.) and I remember I was the second last person to leave every day

SHAY: yeah yeah it doesn't because you have to work

ROSE: you have to ring (.) yeah

SHAY: and um=

ROSE: =if people don't come (Shay, EC, second interview, NS2)

Moving away from 'who' is speaking to 'what' is said shifts focus of analysis on to 'how' what is said was possible. This relates to how the 'things said' are constituted within discursive practices that function in certain ways and the practices of research interviews (Bonham & Bacchi, 2017). Moreover, the subjects of policy are not 'just' wielders of policy but embedded within, constituted by, and enact policy (Gill, 2012). The interviewee is trying to find their footing in their changing workspaces, with a new service delivery model, under a new government contract, with the interviewer joining in and reflecting on past work practices. It highlights the underlying discursive practices of spatializing employment services – and the related component of temporalising employment services. Both of these are, at first, highlighted through employment consultant-participants (and the interviewer-employment consultant) 'describing' their work practices in the interview.

Regarding what is said, the interview/ee are sharing stories about being in understaffed workspace. The problem of being understaffed in the text is constituted as overworking, measured against the time available in a single workday – for example, the measurement of time highlighted by the (lack of a) lunch break. Regarding what is linked to an 'insider's knowledge', the interviewer lists various daily tasks: what it is like to run training sessions, one-on-one case management appointments, job search groups sessions, using the database programs (government database and independent programs), shared work and organisational knowledges. The interviewer shared their 'insider story' and thus reproduces the typical way of talking about work as an employment services worker or at least a typical way presented in the text as the interviewee expresses shared sentiment. The 'employment consultant' here is constituted as a subject inundated with administrative processes, stressed and overworked.

The reference to 'if people do not come' refers to the practice of 'resulting'. Here, the diary of scheduled appointments (one-on-one, group training, group job search) requires a 'result' entered into the government database program by the close of each working day (Department of Employment, 2015). If a client does not attend an appointment, the employment consultant must make contact to find the reason for non-attendance – or at least attempt to make contact. Hence, the agreement between the interviewer and interviewee is that it takes a long time to complete this process before the end of the working day. In the above transcript, the clients are briefly referred to, "if people do not come". In one quick reading, then it seems the transcript does not include a discussion about the unemployed.

However, clients are still always present as the implicit 'other'. There are no training programs without attendees; there is no 'appointment' if there is no client sitting on the other side of the desk. While the organisational practices of understaffing offices are put forward as a cause for the problem of being overworked, the client is also, implicitly, connected. At the same time, 'resulting' may seem like a simple (and annoying) administrative procedure. There are nevertheless lived effects for clients (see Chapter Four). Simple office procedures then are entangled with policy and legislation and have consequences for people's lives.

The sharing of 'insider' stories could open up the discussion of how the workers feel in these situations. However, such a move is political because it might naturalise the discussed practices and the subjectivities being constituted within. Discussing the stress of having to say behind to 'result' the diary could be discussed without considering the wider policy implications for the unemployed, as mentioned above. The 'insider' status helped to co-construct stories about 'what it is like' to 'be' an employment consultant. The 'insider/outsider' practice is situated within the broader discursive practices that constitute (and are constituted by) employment services. However, much of what is said in interviews is nothing more than what was expected or at least did not appear to be anything 'new', beyond common sense. The (re)production of common knowledge is illuminating since "both the interviewer and interviewee are produced within the discursive practices that make possible these things said" (Bonham & Bacchi, 2017, p. 8). In other words, the process of doing interviews has political and ethical implications for the types of subject positions available and the type of 'knowledge' produced.

Concluding comments

Proponents of the 'ontological turn' attest that this research approach "moves us past unresolvable epistemological battles" (Bacchi, 2012, p. 150) and instead focuses on the political implications of the research. This chapter used a critical reflexive lens to highlight some challenges, shortcomings and omissions in critical research. My research was not 'action' oriented, but it was nevertheless still doing something since, as we know from the power-knowledge nexus, research produces knowledge about our world, who we are and how we are able to think about ourselves. I agree with Bacchi (2012) that turning to ontological politics does not upend research. It does not leave us in a relativist void where no knowledge production is 'useful'. Instead, it demands that we pay *more* attention to our practices, especially in light of institutional pressures and expectations to think about "the realities [researchers] create and to assess the political fallout accompanying those realities" (p. 152). 'Ideas', 'concepts' and 'knowledges' intervene in the world in terms of practices, but can they interfere? As Deleuze and Guattari (1988) explained, we can use concepts such as bricks to build a wall or smash a window. The challenge that I have tried to address in my research, but especially in this chapter, is the 'brick' problem. Specifically, we need to think carefully about *how* we produce knowledge lest we unwittingly reinscribe a (meta)theoretical position that we wanted to contest, we (may) end up helping to build the wall. I have argued in this chapter for critical unemployment research that we need to think seriously about our methods and our research's implications. Method(ologies) matter. I summarise the key points of the book in the final chapter.

Notes

1 GROUP, that removed individualised case management, or heart-to-heart conversations, see Chapter Five for more detail.
2 Participants were alerted to this aspect of the interviews before starting, and occasionally a more 'private' space in the office was available for our recorded discussions.

References

Bacchi, C. (2012). Strategic interventions and ontological politics: Research as political practice. In A. Bletsas & C. Beasley's (Eds.), *Engaging with Carol Bacchi: Strategic Interventions with Exchanges*. University of Adelaide Press.

Bonham, J., & Bacchi, C. (2017). Cycling 'subjects' in *ongoing-formation*: The politics of interviews and interview analysis. *Journal of Sociology, 53*(3), 687–703. 10.1177/1440783317715805

Brady, M. (2016). Neoliberalism, governmental assemblages, and the ethnographic imaginary. In M. Brady & R. K. Lippert (Eds.), *Governing Practices: Neoliberalism, Governmentality and the Ethnographic Imaginary*. University of Toronto Press.

Braun, V., & Clarke, V. (2021). Can I use TA? Should I use TA? Should I not use TA? Comparing reflexive thematic analysis and other pattern-based qualitative analytic approaches. *Counselling and Psychotherapy Research, 21*(1), 37–47.

Brinkmann, S. (2013). *Qualitative interviewing: Understanding qualitative research*. Oxford.

Brinkmann, S., & Kvale, S. (2018). *Doing interviews* (2nd edition). SAGE.

Britzman, D. P. (2000). 'The question of belief': Writing poststructural ethnography. In E. St Pierre & W. S. Pillow (Eds.), *Working the Ruins: Feminist Poststructural Theory Methods and Education*. Routledge.

Burman, E. (2017). From subjectification to subjectivity in education policy research relationships. In J. Lester, C. Lochmiller, & R. Gabriel (Eds.), *Discursive Perspectives on Education Policy and Implementation*. Palgrave Macmillan.

Cairns, K. (2013). Ethnographic locations: The geographies of feminist poststructural ethnography. *Ethnography and Education, 8*(3), 323–337.

Collier, S. J. (2013, November). 'Fieldwork as technique for generating what kind of surprise? Thoughts on Post-Soviet Social in light of "Fieldwork/Research"'. Presented at University of California, Irvine, Department of Anthropology, Retrieved from https://stephenjcollier.files.wordpress.com/2014/05/fieldwork-and-surprise.pdf

Creswell, J. W. (2013). *Qualitative inquiry and research design: Choosing among five approaches* (3rd edition). SAGE.

Deleuze, G., & Guattari, F. (1988). *A thousand Plateaus: Capitalism and Schizophrenia*. University of Minnesota Press.

Department of Employment. (2015). Jobactive Deed 2015–2020. Accessed 25 September 2015 from https://docs.employment.gov.au/documents/final-jobactive-deed-2015–2020.

Fadyl, J. K., & Nicholls, D. A. (2013). Foucault, the subject and the interview: A critique of methods. *Nursing Inquiry, 20*(1), 23–29. https://pubmed.ncbi.nlm.nih.gov/23176320/

Fetterman, D. M. (2019). *Ethnography: Step-by-step*. SAGE.

Fine, M. (1994). Working the hyphens: Reinventing self and other in qualitative research. In N. Denzin & Y. Lincoln (Eds.), *Handbook of Qualitative Research*. SAGE.

Foley, L. J. (2012). Constructing the respondent. In J. Gubrium, J. Holstein, A. Marvasti, & K. McKinney (Eds.), *The SAGE Handbook of Interview Research: The Complexity of the Craft* (pp. 305–317). SAGE.

Fontana, A., & Frey, J. H. (2005). The interview: From neutral stance to political involvement. In N. K. Denzin & Y. S. Lincoln (Eds.), *The Sage Handbook of Qualitative Research* (3rd edition) (pp. 695–728). SAGE.

Forsey, M. G. (2010). Ethnography as participant listening, *Ethnography, 11*(4), 58–572. 10.1177/1466138110372587

Foucault, M. (1982). Space, knowledge, power. In J. D. Faubion, (Ed.), *Essential Works, Power, Volume 3* (pp. 349–364). The New Press.

Foucault, M. (2002). *The archaeology of knowledge* (trans. by Alan Sheridan). Taylor & Francis Ltd (Originally published in 1972).

Foucault, M. (2003). The subject and power. In P. Rabinow & N. Rose (Eds.), *The Essential Foucault: Selections from Essential Works of Foucault, 1954–1984* (pp. 126–144). The New York Press.

Frith, H., & Gleeson, K. (2011). Qualitative data collection: Asking the right questions. In D. Harper & A. R. Thompson (Eds.), *Qualitative Research Methods in Mental Health and Psychotherapy: A Guide for Students and Practitioners*. John Wiley & Sons Inc.

Gill, Z. (2012). Located subjects: The daily lives of policy workers. In A. Blatsas & C. Beasley (Eds.), *Engaging with Carol Bacchi: Strategic Interventions and Exchanges*. University of Adelaide Press.

Glaser, B. G., & Strauss, A. L. (1967). T*he discovery of grounded theory: Strategies for qualitative research*. Aldine.

Gobo, G. (2008). *Doing ethnography*. SAGE.

Gubrium, J., & Holstein, J. (2016). Narrative practice and the active interview. In D. Silverman (Ed.), *Qualitative Data Analysis* (pp. 67–82). SAGE.

Herzog, H. (2012). Interview location and its social meaning. In J. F. Gubrium, J. A. Holstein, A. B. Marvasti, & K.D. McKinney (Eds.), *The SAGE Handbook of Interview Research: The Complexity of the Craft*. Sage.

Kerr, R., & Sturm, D. (2019). Moving beyond 'insider or outsider': The ethnographic challenges of researching elite sport facilities in New Zealand. *Qualitative Inquiry, 25*(9–10), 1137–1147.

Laing, A. (2008). *Changing disabling places*. Unpublished PhD thesis. University of Stirling.

Larner, W. (2008). Comments on Stenson's 'Governing the local: Sovereignty, social governance and community safety'. *Social Work and Society – International Online Journal, 6*(1), 21–25. Retrieved from http://www.socwork.net/sws/article/view/87/376.

Mol, A. (1999). Ontological politics: A word and some questions. In J. Law & J. Hassard (Eds.), *Actor Network Theory and After*. Blackwell.

McGrath, C., Palmgren, P. J., & Liljedahl, M. (2018). Twelve tips for conducting qualitative research interviews. *Medical Teacher*, 41, 1002–1006. 10.1080/0142159x.2018.1497149.

Parker, I. (2005). *Qualitative psychology: Introducing radical research*. Open University Press.

Pillow, W. S. (2015). Reflexivity as interpretation and genealogy in research. *Cultural Studies ↔ Critical Methodologies, 15*(6), 419–434. 10.1177/1532708615615605

Rasmussen, J. (2013). Governing the workplace or the worker? Evolving dilemmas in chemical professionals' discourse on occupational health and safety. *Discourse & Communication*, 7(1), 75–94. 10.1177/1750481312466473

Roulston, K. (2010). Considering quality in qualitative interviewing. *Qualitative Research, 10*(2), 199–228. 10.1177/1468794109356739

St Pierre, E. A., & Jackson, A. Y. (2014). Qualitative data analysis after coding. *Qualitative Inquiry, 20*(6), 715–719. 10.1177/1077800414532435

Subramani, S. (2019). Practising reflexivity: Ethics, methodology and theory construction. *Methodological Innovations.* 10.1177/2059799119863276

Tanggaard, L. (2007). The research interview as discourses crossing swords: The researcher and apprentice on crossing roads. *Qualitative Inquiry, 13*(1), 160–176. doi:10.1177/1077800406294948.

Toulmin, S. E. (2003). *The uses of argument.* Cambridge University Press.

Wang, C., & Burris, M. A. (1997). Photovoice: Concept, methodology, and use for participatory needs assessment. *Health Education and Behaviour, 24*(3), 369–387.

Wengraf, T. (2001). *Qualitative research interviewing.* Sage.

7

CONCLUSION

Introduction

This volume draws on an Australian case study to illustrate how punitive activation strategies in employment services utilise individualised and psychologised knowledges and practices that ignore the structural and social factors that constitute unemployment. I also argued that analysis must go beyond understanding the distress of the unemployed as "symptoms of mental ill-health" (Walker et al., 2014, p. 55) to instead see the "distress" and other states of being unemployed as socially constituted. To draw on medical anthropologists, I suggest research on unemployment should study "how inner processes are reshaped amid economic and political reforms, violence and social suffering" (Biehl et al., 2007, p. 1).

In this book, I outlined a non-disciplinary approach to study the (re)constitution of the unemployed 'inner self'. I assembled components from critical psychology, social science, post-Foucauldian research, affective research and ethnography to study the broader processes and daily practices that (re)produce unemployment as a certain type of problem and object. In Chapter Four, I traced a form of 'unemployment' that reshaped the passive and despairing unemployed through increasing conditionality. That conditionality involves blaming the unemployed for their misery of their unemployment, and subsequent financial deprivation.

In Chapter Five, I examined employment consultants daily work to unpack how affective governing practices, produced through interviews and observations, make a limited selection of subject positions available for unemployed clients *and* workers. The inner lives or emotions of clients and workers are constituted as a site where activation is targeted. I borrowed from D'Aoust (2013) to show how 'emotion', as a 'heart' technology illuminated how psy-infused knowledge informed, activated and sustained the 'deficit' unemployed subject, re-enforcing the discourses about the moral imperative to 'activate' people into looking for paid

DOI: 10.4324/9781003112518-7

work, redolent in the government's own policy, *jobactive*, implying that if one is long-term unemployed, one is not 'active enough' in finding a job.

Although the 'experience' of unemployment is partially constituted through the *jobactive* apparatus, the behaviour of employment consultants, and the governmentality utilised in all aspects of interaction with those who are unemployed, psychologises unemployment. This approach maintains that the unemployed are the problem over and above any social, political or economic explanations. Punitive activation and affective governing strategies are oppressive insofar as the interventions try to (re)shape the unemployed into the ideal neoliberal affective subject. This may well be the actions of a "well-intentioned society" (Young, 1988, p. 272), but such an approach, as I have shown, also sustains disadvantage and suffering. A critical approach to unemployment should aim to trouble such practices through exploring how these practices are historically and culturally contingent, but also how they manifest in different spaces, including policy and at the street-level, with varying implications for the unemployed. This is contrary to psychological research that may look at individualised explanations for unemployment misery or seek solutions that are aimed at reforming individual conditions or coping strategies, psychologising and individualising unemployment, detaching it from its political, economic and social formations (see Chapters Three and Four). To examine unemployment in this way requires tackling epistemic issues, including the role of the psy-complex and research practices in constituting and governing unemployment.

Governing unemployment and the psy-complex

Embedded within activation discourses is the idea that "the best form of welfare is a job" (Abbott, 2015). These 'work-first' discursive practices situate paid employment as crucial to individual and social wellbeing by diminishing the welfare state's responsibilities and the citizens' right to access its services minus the stigma of shame. As I argued in Chapter Four, these practices instead equate 'wellbeing' with work or, at least, *looking for* work. In Chapter Three, I highlighted how psy-complexified knowledges about the meaning of work and the integral role of work to maintain 'subjective wellbeing' have become 'common sense' (see also Fryer, 2019). These psy-infused ideas about the importance of productivism mean paid employment takes on a moral aspect by being the institution where 'mental health' is maintained and potentially improved. Such arguments resonate in other Global North contexts (see Sage, 2018; McKenna et al., 2019).

Similarly, the idea of work-as-welfare is reproduced in research that 'documents' the detrimental consequences unemployment has on 'emotional wellbeing' (Wood & Burchell, 2018). As I showed in Chapter Four, ES policy and practices assumed work to be 'therapeutic' justifying the need to 'hassle' to 'help'. Unemployed subjectivities need to be reshaped so people are 'job ready' and 'get well', or at least, not get worse. The *jobactive* apparatus' "urgent need" (Foucault, 1980, p. 194) is to ensure citizens participate in the labour market and take responsibility for their wellbeing. On the flipside of this argument, the 'passive welfare state' creates welfare dependency and is, therefore, "letting job seekers down" (Abbott, 2015). 'Psychopolitics' entangles the labour market and mental health to legitimise welfare policy (Sandle et al., 2018), making it difficult to contest since to do so would mean also rejecting the idea that (re)employment is good for society *and* the individual.

The challenge is how to resist practices of punitive activation without re-inscribing the pscyhopolitics about work and welfare. Psychological notions of unemployment may be deployed as a tactic to contest the problematic practices within employment services. However, this strategy, albeit sometimes useful (Fryer, 2012), is also 'dangerous'. It is 'dangerous' because it provides a different set of governing practices that subjectify people in certain psychological, individual and normalised ways (Rose, 1996). It connects to policy nodes and other governing practices that weaponise 'affect' to deter or discourage people from accessing welfare (Mills & Klein, 2021). Crucially, individualising/psychologising unemployment makes invisible the other possible ways of understanding, and thereby 'experiencing', unemployment. Research needs to find a way to trouble and transcend this pervasive thinking.

The problem of pervasive thinking

As argued in Chapter Two, an integral aspect of Foucauldian-inspired research is to uncover possibilities for being otherwise (Foucault, 2003b). Part of looking for these modes of resistance or escape comes from examining *what* is said but also in recognising the political (potential) of research insofar as there are always multiple reading of the text and presented readings diminish other possible interpretations (Bonham & Bacchi, 2017). In the fieldwork discussed in Chapter Five, there was a possible reading of the transcripts that the workers problematised work-first discourses by drawing on psychologised discourses. Interviewees discussed introducing the 'heart' technologies through increasing participation via 'career' brainstorming exercises or lamenting the loss of affective governing strategies to defuse anger. However, the psychologising of unemployment through emotions maintained the individualisation of unemployment, albeit more emotionally complex than the SDP allows. Holding onto these assumed subjectivities, in essence, did not subvert the assumption that *jobactive*, and employment services, can 'solve' the 'problem' of 'unemployment'. The emphasis on needing affective governing strategies via 'heart' technologies maintained the pervasive thinking that economic participation is, and should be, the goal of a 'good' and 'responsible' citizen. This book therefore questioned the assumption that psychologising unemployment through case management practices can soften or transform activation.

This book also took seriously how 'unemployment' is produced as an object (Parker, 2005) and how research intervenes in the world (Mol, 1999). From my examination of the method of psy and governmentality (see Chapter Three) and my research (see Chapter Six), I argue that critical unemployment researchers should examine the politics of how research is *done* when researching governing practices and with what implications. In my research, the mundane practices of doing research, such as building rapport by sharing work experiences, (re)produced dominant discourses about unemployment.

The research interviews were reflexively examined for how they reproduced pervasive thinking and discourses about unemployment. I started with the assumption that interviews could be useful because they are constituted through and help to think about the multiplicity of power relations, and accordingly, are also open for transformation (Bonham & Bacchi, 2017). Interviews can help to analyse otherness while also opening up lines of inquiry for potential transformation. I found this was not an either/or practice. In moments where I managed to problematise dominant practices or interviewees challenged the work-first practices, psychological discourses were deployed in ways that sustained pervasive thinking about the problem of unemployment. This came from interviewees and the researcher and was inseparable from the methods used. The unemployed were assumed to lack imagined qualities of the employed. Contesting work-first discourses through the psy-complex both reproduced the unemployed as deficit and psychologised unemployment because psy-complexified knowledges provided the expertise on who needed 'help', if they could be 'helped', and how to do the 'helping'.

Psy and employment services post-COVID: Final comments

The COVID-19 pandemic did not overturn welfare regimes, although it did provide glimpses of what could be possible. The pandemic illuminated the important role that social security protection plays in contemporary society. Global North welfare regimes such as Australia's, were temporarily reformed by taking responsibility for the welfare of the un/der/employed, stood down workers and workers without enough, or any, hours. Various countries instigated income transfers, wage subsidies or softened and sometimes suspended welfare conditionality for the un/der/employed or those workers who were at risk of becoming so (see IMF, n.d.). In Australia, a wage subsidy for workers and a COVID supplement for the unemployed (among a raft of other practices such as free childcare) demonstrated very clearly that the government could rethink the work-welfare nexus (Treasury, 2020). With everyone affected, there was little ability to pathologise through policy those stood down due to the pandemic.

Research internationally and in Australia has shown that softening welfare regimes and activation practices during the pandemic improved people's lives. People had more money to buy necessities, such as medication, ate more healthily and stressed less about housing (Australian Council of Social Services, 2020). Other research showed that taking the pressure of finding work allowed people to pursue interests and explore other work possibilities in Denmark (Pultz et al., 2021), improved health outcomes in the United States and Israel (Gal & Madhaha, 2021; Miraniahangarkolaei, et al., 2021) or take time to engage in other important social practices such as caring (Klein et al., 2021). In Australia, the suspension of mutual obligations lasted until September 2020 and the COVID supplement was removed in March 2021. As different parts of Australia went into lockdown to curb the infection rate in 2021, workers who lost hours received state support but the unemployed did not. The government's claims that they were supporting all Australians early on in the pandemic dissipated into blame-the-unemployed-as-usual, regurgitating outdated and discredited arguments about the 'welfare bludger', 'replacements rates' and evoking 'individual responsibility' to look for work (Stambe & Marston, in press).

As I write this conclusion, Australia's welfare state has returned to a pre-pandemic normal. The focus now is on moving towards a digitalised model, lessening direct contact between ES workers and 'job-ready' clients but intensifying support for those less 'job ready'. Concern has been raised about the unintended consequences of increased digital surveillance in the panoptic toolkit governing poverty (Staines et al., 2020) and for vulnerable clients such as young single mothers (Casey, 2021). Once again the focus is on 'how best to govern' via these intensive interventions that are supposedly driven by big data to recommend "what works best" and disseminate "evidence-based tools" to assist providers to drive the "best outcomes" (Department of Jobs and Small Business, 2018, p. 53). Again, commentators recommend the current pilots focus on personalised services utilising psy-based expertise (such as social work) (Casey & Lewis 2020). The Government is showing no sign of softening punitive activation practices. In this scenario, any evidence-based practices, psychological or otherwise, will be tied to welfare conditionality, and therefore, also connected to discourses about citizenship, activation and economic participation. The momentum and learnings about what is possible when the out of work are provided adequate financial help without the hassle is going to waste.

A critical approach to unemployment should refuse micro-level activation that rely on psychological concepts, intervention or assumptions about the self that are part of the apparatus and objectify unemployment as a problem of passive and faulty citizens. This endeavour involves moving past concepts such as 'depression' and 'self-esteem' to broaden and politise our understanding of 'harm' and 'wellbeing'. As I have discussed, the 'affective turn' holds potential to think seriously about the unemployed's distress without relying on psy-complexified concepts that pathologise socially constituted misery. There are two ongoing concerns here, however. Firstly, the affective turn can still (re)psy-complexify distress by treating emotions/affects as *essential* to understanding distress without seeing it as part of a larger social and cultural assemblage (Gorman, 2017). Secondly, affective governing does not subjectify people homogeneously (Fortier, 2016). Such diverse practices and impacts should be considered seriously, such as how practices to 'help' the unemployed in different welfare regimes are classed, gendered and racialised (Abramovitz, 2006; Montenegro & Montenegro, 2013, Wright & Patrick, 2019).

A limitation of my research is that it did not capture the diversity of the unemployed people the workers were supposedly activating. I focused on workers for interviews to highlight the front-line problematisation alongside policy and missed interrogating which clients were targeted, consequently also homogenising the unemployed. This is a limitation of my research because while it is true that unemployment manifests in different types of economies and is governed differently depending on social/policy context, in Australia governing practices are also deployed unevenly across the unemployed cohort. Notably, Aboriginal and Torres Strait Islander peoples have higher unemployment rates and are disproportionately targeted with punitive activation strategies, such as income management (Marston et al., 2020). Future research could integrate an intersectional lens with governing research by foregrounding how power relations in these spaces are dispersed, without reintroducing psy-complexified notions of the self. Additionally, further research could explore how elements such as class, gender and race intersect with emotions, affects and feelings to constitute how people can experience 'unemployment'. Future research should focus on specific emotions such as 'depression' to detail how unemployment, as a fluid, social, historical, economic and political practice, can 'feel' 'depressing' thus illuminating how our inner processes are in the state of 'becoming-other' from the institutional, political and social reforms and practices that constitute the lives we can live.

An ongoing challenge is how to research such gaps and concerns without reinscribing pervasive thinking. Foucauldian-inspired research usefully helps to trouble taken-for-granted assumptions to the point that it becomes difficult to let things continue as they are (Foucault, 2003c). It evokes a "hyper-and pessimistic activism" (Foucault, 2003d, p. 104) but, as a tool, is unable to prescribe an alternative way forward or path of action. Accordingly. I recognise that more socially engaged and culturally responsive activism/research may be more relevant in another contexts, particularly in the Global South or with indigenous peoples (Hodgetts et al., 2020; see, for example, Dudgeon et al., 2020). Participatory and activist research may be one way forward to reclaim the potential to rethink unemployment and social protection and the work-welfare nexus. There have been interesting participatory studies that engage in activism with and for the unemployed in the United Kingdom (Ploetner et al., 2020), including activist/union-type organisations in Australia (O'Halloran et al., 2020). These studies suggest a more 'ground up' approach working alongside those without work could fruitfully challenge the governing of the unemployed and address the gaps I mentioned previously. However, there are tensions between participatory and governmentality research in terms of purpose and underpinning assumptions about the self, the social world and the purpose of research that need unpacking and reworking (Stambe & Fryer, 2014). At the end of this book, I concede that the constant interrogation of methods means none are satisfactory, but I do not want to suggest that we get so bogged down in problematising methods that we become paralysed (Bridges-Rhoads, 2015). In these COVID times where the potential to rethink how we 'solve' the 'problem' of unemployed has been missed, we need to somehow engage as activist-researchers and continue to struggle through the (meta)theoretical incoherence and tension to rethink unemployment and refuse to blame the unemployed.

References

Abbott, T. (2015). *New jobactive service to help more jobseekers into work.* (Press release) Retrieved from https://www.pm.gov.au/media/2015-03-31/new-jobactive-services-help-more-jobseekers-work.

Abramovitz, M. (2006). Welfare reform in the United States: Gender, race and class matter. *Critical Social Policy, 26*(2), 336–364.

Australian Council of Social Services (ACOSS). (2020). *I can finally eat fresh fruit and vegetables survey of 955 people receiving the new rate of jobseeker and other allowances.* ACOSS.

Biehl, J., Good, B., & Kleinman, A. (2007). *Subjectivity: Ethnographic investigations.* University of California Press.

Bonham, J., & Bacchi, C. (2017). Cycling subjects' in ongoing-formation: The politics of interviews and interview analysis. *Journal of Sociology, 53*(3), 687–703. 10.1177/1440783317715805

Bridges-Rhoads, S. (2015). Writing paralysis in (post) qualitative research. *Qualitative Inquiry, 21*(8), 704–710. 10.1177/1077800414566690

Casey, S. J. (2021). *Towards digital dole parole: A review of digital self-service initiatives in Australian employment services.* Australian Journal of Social Issues.

Casey, S. J., & Lewis, A. (2020). Redesigning employment services after COVID-19. Per Capita. Retrieved from Redesigning Employment Services after COVID-19 – Per Capita.

D'Aoust, A. (2013). In the name of love: Marriage migration, governmentality and technologies of love. *International Political Sociology*, 7, 258–274. 10.1111/ips.12022

Department of Jobs and Small Business. (2018, December). I want to work: Employment Services Report 2020. Retrieved from advisory-panel-report-i-want-work-employment-services-2020.

Dudgeon, P., Bray, A., Darlaston-Jones, D., & Walker, R. (2020). Aboriginal participatory action research: An indigenous research methodology strengthening decolonisation and social and emotional wellbeing. (Lowitja Institute Discussion Paper Series). The Lowitja Institute. https://www.lowitja.org.au/content/Document/Lowitja-Publishing/LI_Discussion_Paper_P-Dudgeon_FINAL3.pdf

Fortier, A. (2016). Afterword: Acts of affective citizenship? Possibilities and limitations. *Citizenship Studies, 20*(8), 1038–1044, 10.1080/13621025.2016.1229190

Foucault, M. (1980). Confessions of the flesh. In C. Gordon (Ed.), *Power/knowledge: Selected interviews and other writings, 1972–1977.* Pantheon Books.

Foucault, M. (2003a). The ethics of the concern of the self as a practice of freedom. In P. Rabinow & N. Rose (Eds.), *The Essential Foucault: Selections from Essential Works of Foucault, 1954–1984* (pp. 25–41). The New York Press.

Foucault, M. (2003b). What is critique? In P. Rabinow & N. Rose (Eds.), *The Essential Foucault: Selections from Essential Works of Foucault, 1954–1984* (pp. 263–278). The New York Press.

Foucault, M. (2003c). So it is important to think? In P. Rabinow & N. Rose (Eds.), *The Essential Foucault: Selections from Essential Works of Foucault, 1954–1984* (pp. 170–173). The New York Press.

Foucault, M. (2003d). On the genealogy of ethics: An overview of work in progress. In P. Rabinow & N. Rose (Eds.), *The Essential Foucault: Selections from Essential Works of Foucault, 1954–1984* (pp. 102–125). The New York Press.

Fryer, D. (2012). Critical differences: The development of a community critical psychological perspective on the psychological costs of unemployment. In T. Kieselbach & S. Mannila (Eds.), *Unemployment, Precarious Work and Health: Research and Policy Issues* (pp. 473–489). Springer.

Fryer, D. (2019). Applied social psychology, the neoliberal labour-market subject and critique. In K. Doherty & D. Hodgetts (Eds.), *The SAGE Handbook of Applied Social Psychology*. SAGE.

Gal, J., & Madhala, S. (2021). The social welfare system and the coronavirus crisis: An overview. https://www.taubcenter.org.il/wp-content/uploads/2021/01/thesocialwelfaresystemandthecoronaviruscrisisanoverviewеng.pdf

Gorman, R. (2017). Quagmies of affect: Madness, labour, whiteness, and ideolgoical disavowal. American Quarterly, *69*(2), 309–313.

Hodgetts, D., Sonn, C., Li, W., & Groot, S. (2020). What does Theory & Psychology have to offer community-orientated psychologists? *Theory & Psychology, 30*(6), 852–863. 10.1177/0959354320947821

International Monetary Fund. (n.d.). Policy responses to COVID-19 – Policy tracker. Retrieved 26 October 2021 from https://www.imf.org/en/Topics/imf-and-covid19/Policy-Responses-to-COVID-19

Klein, E., Cook, K., Maury, S., & Bowey, K. (2021). *Social security and time use during COVD-19*. 10.25916/yetx-9m76.

Marston, G., Mendes, P., Bielefeld, S., Peterie, M., Staines, Z., & Roche, S. (2020). *Hidden costs: An independent study into income management in Australia*. https://www.incomemanagementstudy.com/blog/hiddencosts

McKenna, D., Peters, P., & Moth, R. (2019). Resisting the work cure: Mental health, welfare reform and the movement against psychocompulsion. In M. Berghs, T. Chataika, Y. El-Lahib, & K. Dube (Eds.), *The Routledge Handbook of Disability Activism* (pp. 128–143). Routledge.

Miraniahangarkolaei, M., Demir, E., Constantinou, T., Toranji, M., & Adino, T. (2021). Job destruction, unemployment, and unemployment insurance benefits: Evidence from the outbreak of COVID-19 across US Counties. Available at SSRN: https://ssrn.com/abstract=3762663 or 10.2139/ssrn.3762663

Mol, A. (1999). Ontological politics: A word and some questions. In J. Law & J. Hassard, (Eds.), *Actor Network Theory and After*. Blackwell.

Mills , C., & Klein, E. (2021). Affective technologies of welfare deterrence in Australia and the United Kingdom. *Economy & Society, 50*(3), 397-422. 10.1080/03085147.2021.1875692

Montenegro, K., & Montenegro, M. (2013). Governmentality in service provision for migrated women in Spain. *Social and Personality Psychology Compass*, 7(6), 331–342.

O'Halloran, D., Farnworth, L., & Thomacos, N. (2020). Australian employment services: Help or hindrance in the achievement of mutual obligation?. *Australian Journal of Social Issues, 55*(4), 492–508.

Parker, I. (2005). *Qualitative psychology: Introducing radical research*. Open University Press.

Ploetner, C., Telford, M., Brækkan, K., Mullen, K., Turnbull, S., Gumley, A., & Allan, S. (2020). Understanding and improving the experience of claiming social security for mental health problems in the west of Scotland: A participatory social welfare study. *Journal of Community Psychology, 48*(3), 675–692. 10.1002/jcop.22278

Pultz, S., Hansen, M. P., & Jepsen, H. (2021). Planning for a job: The trying experience of unemployment during the COVID-19 crisis in Denmark. *International Perspectives in Psychology: Research, Practice, Consultation, 10*(4), 228–272. 10.1027/2157-3891/a000028

Rose, N. (1996). *Inventing ourselves: Psychology, power and personhood*. Cambridge University Press.

Sage, D. (2018). Wellbeing and the welfare state. In B. Greve (Ed.), *Routledge Handbook of the Welfare State* (pp. 101–112). Routledge.

Staines, Z., Moore, C., Marston, G., & Humpage, L. (2020). Big data and poverty governance under Australia and Aotearoa/New Zealand's social investment policies. *Australian Journal of Social Issues*, *56*, 16. 10.1002/ajs4.129

Stambe, R., & Fryer, D. (2014). Photovoice: Doing assessed research as an undergraduate from a critical standpoint. *SAGE Research Method Cases*. Retrieved from 10.4135/978144627305013509770

Stambe, R., & Marston, G. (in press). Checking activation at the door: Rethinking the welfare-work nexus in light of Australia's COVID-19 response. *Social Policy & Society*.

Sandle, R. V., Day, K., & Muskett, T. (2018). Working to feel better or feeling better to work? Discourses of wellbeing in Austerity reality TV. *Review of Disability Studies: An International Journal*, *14*(2), 1–19. https://rdsjournal.org/index.php/journal/article/view/821.

Treasury. (2020). *Economic response to the coronavirus*. Retrieved from https://treasury.gov.au/coronavirus

Walker, C., Hanna, P., Cunningham, L., & Ambrose, P. (2014). A kind of mental warfare: An economy of affect in the UK debt collection industry. *The Australian Community Psychologist*, *26*(2), 54–67.

Wood, A. J., & Burchell, B. J. (2018). Unemployment and wellbeing. In A. Lewis (Ed.), *Cambridge Handbook of Psychological and Economic Behaviour* (2nd edition) (pp. 234–259). Cambridge University Press.

Wright, S., & Patrick, R. (2019). Welfare conditionality in lived experience: Aggregating qualitative longitudinal research. *Social Policy & Society*, *18*(4), 597–613.

Young, M. I. (1988). Five faces of oppression. *The Philosophical Forum*, *19*(4), 270–290.

INDEX

For Product Safety Concerns and Information please contact our EU representative GPSR@taylorandfrancis.com Taylor & Francis Verlag GmbH, Kaufingerstraße 24, 80331 München, Germany